THE GOOGLE AD GRANT ULTIMATE GUIDE

Featuring 45+ Case Studies

Table of Contents

INTRODUCTION	1
CHAPTER 1 — WHAT IS THE GOOGLE AD GRANT?	5
The Essence of the Google Ad Grant	5
Eligibility Requirements	6
Applying for the Grant	6
Key Features and Limitations	7
Who is a good fit for Google Ad Grants?	7
Potential Use Cases	8
Why Does the Average Grantee Only Spend $800/month?	9
Conclusion	10
Understanding the Basics of Keywords	11
CHAPTER 2 — KEYWORD RESEARCH STRATEGY	11
Conducting Thorough Keyword Research	12
Developing a Keyword Strategy	13
Conclusion	14
Structuring Your Ad Campaigns	15
CHAPTER 3 — CREATING EFFECTIVE AD CAMPAIGNS	15
Writing Compelling Ad Copy	16
Utilizing Ad Extensions	17
Best Practices for Google Ad Grant Campaigns	18
Conclusion	18

CHAPTER 4 — LANDING PAGE OPTIMIZATION   20

Understanding the Role of Landing Pages. 20
Key Elements of High-Converting Landing Pages 21
Optimizing Landing Pages for Conversions 22
Measuring and Analyzing Landing Page Performance. 22
Conclusion. 23
The Importance of Tracking and Measuring Performance. 25

CHAPTER 5 — TRACKING AND MEASURING PERFORMANCE   25

Setting Up Conversion Tracking 26
Setting Up Conversion Tracking in Google Analytics 4 (GA4). 26
Setting Up Conversion Tracking Using Google Tag Manager 29
Integrating Google Ads and Google Analytics. 32
Analyzing Key Performance Metrics 35
Leveraging Data for Continuous Improvement. 36
Conclusion. 36

CHAPTER 6 — CONTENT MARKETING   38

Understanding Content Marketing Relative to the Google Grant. 38
Types of Content Marketing. 39
The Benefits of Content Marketing 40
Conclusion. 43

CHAPTER 7 — MAINTAINING COMPLIANCE AND AVOIDING COMMON MISTAKES   44

Understanding Google Ad Grant Policies 44
Common Compliance Issues and Solutions 45
Best Practices for Ensuring Compliance 46
Conclusion. 47

CHAPTER 8 — THE IMPACT OF USING A GOOGLE AD GRANTS CERTIFIED PROFESSIONAL AGENCY   48

Understanding Google Ad Grants Certified Professional Agencies. 48
Benefits of Partnering with a Certified Agency. 49
Impact on Nonprofit Organizations. 50
Choosing the Right Certified Agency 50

CASE STUDIES   52

Animal Nonprofit Case Studies 53
Arts & Culture Nonprofit Case Studies 60
Civic & Social Nonprofit Case Studies 64

Education Nonprofit Case Studies 68
 Environmental Nonprofit Case Studies 74
 Health Nonprofit Case Studies. 79
 Human & Civil Rights Nonprofit Case Studies. 84
 Human Services Nonprofit Case Studies 88
 Faith & Religion Nonprofit Case Studies 93
 Sports & Athletics Nonprofit Case Studies 98
 Youth Nonprofit Case Studies. 102

GLOSSARY OF KEY TERMS 104

CONCLUSION 111

Introduction

People search Google for topics related to your nonprofit every hour of every day. Will they find your organization?

Managing the $10,000/month Google Ad Grant for 750+ active client nonprofit organizations gives us a front-row seat to see the impact that reaching people through Google can have. Every person who types anything in the Google search box is looking for *something*. For a brief moment, that question or goal in their mind has their complete attention. Their eyes start at the top of the search results page and scroll downwards, and in that half second of truth, your nonprofit will either be there, ready to help, or educate, or receive support... or not.

Today, less than 10% of the over 1 million registered 501(c)(3) nonprofit organizations in the United States use the Google Grant. But the story of underutilization doesn't stop there. Nonprofits that use the Google Grant receive $10,000 in ad credit each month, yet on average, most will only spend around $800 of that balance-- approximately 8% of its overall potential.

This means that the nonprofit industry, just in the United States, is leaving a staggering $119,040,000,000 of potential Google Grant opportunity on the table *every year*. Not to mention the rest of the world.

This is why we started Nonprofit Megaphone (nonprofitmegaphone.com), a specialized marketing agency that focuses on the Google Ad Grant. We are proud to manage more Google Ad Grants than any other organization in the world. We love the Google Grant program, and it has been deeply meaningful to work closely with Google to help make the program as impactful as it can be.

Nearly all of the nonprofits we talk to are underresourced in one way or another. For those who have some budget, but never enough time, we are thrilled to do all of the heavy lifting to manage their Google Grant. From grant acquisition to writing ads to conversion tracking, reporting, keeping up with platform changes and constant optimization, we ensure that our clients are getting the most of the Grant with hardly any time commitment.

Some organizations, though, are comparatively "rich" in time but constrained in terms of finances. We give our Grant Mangers three full months of full-time training to equip them to manage the Google Grant as effectively as possible.

But in many cases, dedicating that sort of time simply isn't realistic for most nonprofit organizations. Because of these constraints, we've distilled the most important concepts into this book to provide you with an introduction if you'd like to manage the Google Grant yourself. Our main goal is to see nonprofits effectively utilize the Grant program, whatever form that takes.

This book has two distinct sections. The first chapters explain what the Google Grant is, how it works, and what other areas of nonprofit marketing it harmonizes with. Then, to provide a bit of inspiration, we have collected nearly 50 case studies from our clients, showcasing how they use the Google Grant to achieve meaningful impact. Finally, as a reference guide, we have included a Glossary of Key terms that you can always turn to if you need a refresher on Google Grant jargon.

Before we jump into the meat of the book, starting with a quick but deep dive into what the Google Ad Grant is and how it works, I wanted to stay thank you.

On behalf of our whole team, thank you for your commitment to your nonprofit organization, whether you are a staff member, board member, or volunteer. Thank you for seeing a problem or opportunity in the world and taking steps to make things better. You are the rare person who matches actions to words, and who demonstrates through their example what a life of contribution really looks like.

You are the true hero of this story, and we salute you.

With gratitude,

— -Grant Hensel, CEO of Nonprofit Megaphone, and the entire NPM team.

Chapter One

What is the Google Ad Grant?

Before we get into the nuts and bolts of how to maximize the opportunity that the Google Grant presents, let's first take a step back and set the table with an overview of what the Grant actually *is*.

Established in 2003, the Google Ad Grant is a unique philanthropic initiative offered by Google that provides nonprofit organizations with the opportunity to advertise on Google's platform at no cost. This grant is part of Google's broader commitment to supporting nonprofit organizations worldwide, helping them increase their visibility, drive donations, engage volunteers, and expand their impact.

THE ESSENCE OF THE GOOGLE AD GRANT

At its core, the Google Ad Grant is a donation of $10,000 USD per month in advertising credits on Google Ads. This grant enables nonprofits to appear in search results at the moment potential donors or volunteers look for relevant information on Google. The idea is to leverage the power of search engine advertising to promote the nonprofit's mission, events, and initiatives without the burden of traditional advertising costs.

ELIGIBILITY REQUIREMENTS

To qualify for the Google Ad Grant, organizations need to meet the following requirements:

- You must be a 501(c)(3) nonprofit organization in the United States or hold a similar status in one of the 50+ countries that have been added to the program so far.

- Your organization must not be a hospital, school or college, or governmental institution. However, philanthropic arms of educational institutions may still be eligible.

- You must have a high-quality website, complying with Google's Website Policy. The site must also be hosted on your own domain (e.g. "ournonprofit.org," not "ournonprofit.weebly.com").

- If you are applying for the Google Grant for the first time, your website must have an SSL certificate installed (which means that a lock icon appears in the navigation bar in Google Chrome). If you see "not secure" next to your website's URL in Chrome, it means SSL is not installed or there is a configuration issue.

- You must agree to the terms of service for Google for Nonprofits and Google Ads.

APPLYING FOR THE GRANT

The application process involves several steps, starting with the validation of nonprofit status through Google for Nonprofits. Once accepted, organizations must create a Google Ads account and set up their first campaign in compliance with Google's policies. Approval can take a few days to a few weeks, depending on various factors including compliance with guidelines and the completeness of the application.

KEY FEATURES AND LIMITATIONS

Features:

- $10,000 per month (every month!) in search advertising credit
- Ability to run text-based ads on Google search results pages
- Access to Google Ads tools to manage and optimize campaigns

Limitations:

- Ads are text-based and limited to appearing in Google Search (no display ads, YouTube ads, etc.)
- Your advertisements will appear below paid advertisements on Google Search (if an advertiser paying real money advertises on the same keyword, their ad will always appear above a Google Grant ad). Google Grant ads and paid ads look exactly the same to a user searching in Google, but the paid ads will always appear at the top.
- There are a variety of Google Grant compliance rules that must be followed to maintain grant access, which we'll discuss in detail in the following chapters.

WHO IS A GOOD FIT FOR GOOGLE AD GRANTS?

Many organizations, especially smaller nonprofits, question whether they are the right size to take full advantage of the Google Ad Grant. Although applying for a grant with a company as big as Google might seem intimidating, the grant is designed with *all* nonprofits in mind. Just because you have a smaller team doesn't mean that you couldn't benefit from the Google Grant.

The main factors that determine the potential value of the Google Grant for your organization include:

- How many people are searching for the topics that your organization deals with?
- Do you have content on your website that speaks to those topics?

The answers to these questions are not dependent on how large or small your organization may be! Many small nonprofits still serve large audiences and have the website content their target population is looking for. These nonprofits thrive with the Google Ad Grant.

In fact, smaller nonprofits could even gain more benefits. The Google Ad Grant provides ad credit that levels the playing field across nonprofits of all sizes.

POTENTIAL USE CASES

We've explored what the Google Ad Grant is and what it has to offer, but what can that mean in practical terms? It is so much more than just driving traffic to your website! Let's explore a few ways that nonprofit organizations can put Google Ad Grants to work for themselves in more creative and effective capacities.

- Informing and educating the public by attracting new visitors
- Selling tickets for performances, events, and webinars
- Driving in-person actions, such as adopting animals from shelters
- Recruiting volunteers to advance the organization's mission or work on a cause
- Advocating by galvanizing grassroots activism, signing petitions, and contacting elected officials
- Promoting donation and sponsorship opportunities to generate funds

- Building an audience by attracting new subscribers to newsletters

Fully utilizing the Google Ad Grant doesn't end with just increasing web traffic. Instead, using carefully targeted ads can help you promote your events, inform the public, recruit passionate supporters, and bring your organization another step closer to accomplishing your mission. The work you do matters, and this grant helps ensure that your efforts are seen by as many people as possible.

WHY DOES THE AVERAGE GRANTEE ONLY SPEND $800/MONTH?

Despite having access to $10,000/month, the average nonprofit in the program only deploys about 8% of that per month, or $800. Why is that?

We will dig into this in much greater detail in the chapters that follow, but unlike normal "paid" ads accounts, it is genuinely difficult to spend money in a Google Grant account. Because Google Grant ads show up below paid ads, running ads on competitive keywords could mean your ads hardly show at all.

Google also essentially forces you (through their compliance rules, which we'll discuss later) to only run very high quality ads at relevant and targeted audiences. You aren't allowed to use single word keywords (which are incredibly broad) and you can't target geographies that don't make sense for your organization (if you serve one city, it doesn't make sense to target the whole world with your ads). Additionally, you need to have excellent conversion tracking in place to give Google AI-driven bidding strategies enough data to work with on what kinds of people you want to be reaching.

As we'll also discuss in a later chapter, Google also requires you to have a relevant landing page to send anyone clicking on your ads to. As a result, your ad account can be effectively limited by the amount of content you have on your website that people are searching for. If your website only has a home page, a donation page, and an about page, it will be difficult to deploy more than a tiny fraction of the Google Grant. If, on the other hand, you have a robust set of pages on topics that lots of people are searching for (think blog articles like "Benefits of adopting a dog" and not "Highlights from our recent gala"), the Google Grant can become one of the most powerful tools in your digital marketing arsenal.

CONCLUSION

In this chapter, we've laid the groundwork for understanding the Google Ad Grant's potential. The following chapters will delve into the specifics of setting up and managing campaigns, optimizing for maximum impact, and complying with Google's policies to ensure ongoing eligibility and success.

Chapter Two

Keyword Research Strategy

Keyword research and strategy lie at the heart of a successful Google Ad Grant campaign. By identifying the right keywords and phrases that align with your nonprofit's mission and goals, you can attract highly relevant audiences, drive targeted traffic to your website, and maximize the impact of your ad spend. In this chapter, we'll dive deep into the process of conducting effective keyword research and developing a comprehensive strategy tailored to the unique needs of your organization.

UNDERSTANDING THE BASICS OF KEYWORDS

Before we delve into the research process, let's establish a clear understanding of what keywords are and why they matter. In the context of Google Ads, keywords are the words or phrases that users type into the search engine when looking for information, products, or services. When you create an ad campaign, you select specific keywords that trigger your ads to appear in the search results when users search for those terms.

For example, if your nonprofit focuses on animal welfare, some relevant keywords might include "animal rescue," "pet adoption," "spay and neuter services," or "animal cruelty prevention." By targeting these keywords, your ads will be displayed to users who are actively searching for information related to your cause.

CONDUCTING THOROUGH KEYWORD RESEARCH

Effective keyword research involves identifying the terms and phrases that your target audience is using to find information related to your nonprofit's mission. Ultimately, this process helps you uncover valuable insights into the language, intent, and priorities of your potential supporters. Here are some key steps to conducting thorough keyword research:

1. *Brainstorm initial keyword ideas*: Start by brainstorming a list of keywords and phrases that are relevant to your organization's work. Consider your mission statement, core programs, target audience, and unique value proposition. Involve team members from different departments to gather diverse perspectives and ideas.

2. *Use keyword research tools*: Leverage tools like Google Keyword Planner, SEMrush, SpyFu, Answer the Public, or Ahrefs to expand your keyword list and gather data on search volume, competition, and related terms. These tools provide valuable insights into the popularity and relevance of different *Analyze competitor keywords*: Research the keywords that your competitors or similar organizations are targeting. Identify gaps or opportunities to differentiate your approach and capture untapped audiences.

3. *Consider user intent*: Evaluate the intent behind each keyword to ensure alignment with your goals. Are users searching for information, resources, or ways to get involved? Prioritize keywords that match the intent of your target audience.

4. *Refine and group keywords*: Organize your keywords into thematic clusters or ad groups based on common themes or categories. This structure will help you create targeted

ad campaigns and landing pages that resonate with specific audience segments.

DEVELOPING A KEYWORD STRATEGY

With your keyword research complete, it's time to develop a comprehensive strategy that maximizes the impact of your Google Ad Grant. Here are some essential elements to consider:

1. *Prioritize high-impact keywords*: Focus your efforts on keywords that have a strong alignment with your mission, high search volume, and reasonable competition. These keywords are more likely to drive meaningful traffic and engagement.

2. *Use long-tail keywords*: Don't overlook the power of long-tail keywords — longer, more specific phrases that target niche audiences. While they may have lower search volume, long-tail keywords often have higher conversion rates and less competition. Long tail keywords typically are 3+ words long and are used by people searching for very specific information.

3. *Utilize keyword match types*: Google Ads offers different keyword match types (broad, phrase, exact) that control how closely the user's search query must match your chosen keywords. Strategic use of match types allows you to fine-tune your targeting and optimize your budget. For the Google Grant, since budget is rarely an issue, you can typically just stick with broad match to start.

4. *Continuously monitor and refine*: Keyword strategy is an ongoing process. Regularly monitor your campaign performance, identify top-performing keywords, and adjust your strategy based on data-driven insights. Stay attuned to changing search trends and user behaviors to maintain relevance.

CONCLUSION

Keyword research and strategy are essential to a successful Google Ad Grant campaign. By investing time and effort into identifying the right keywords and developing a comprehensive strategy, nonprofits can attract highly relevant audiences, drive targeted traffic, and maximize the impact of their ad spend.

Remember, keyword strategy is an ongoing process that requires continuous monitoring, refinement, and adaptation. Stay attuned to your audience's needs, monitor campaign performance, and make data-driven decisions to optimize your approach.

By mastering the art and science of keyword research and strategy, you'll unlock the full potential of your Google Ad Grant and drive meaningful results for your nonprofit's mission... but it doesn't stop there. In the next chapter, we'll use what we know about keywords to explore the intricacies of creating compelling ad campaigns – the kind that not only capture attention, but that inspire action.

Chapter Three

Creating Effective Ad Campaigns

You have your keywords... now what?

With a solid foundation of keyword research and strategy in place, it's time to dive into the art of crafting effective ad campaigns. Your Google Ad Grant provides a valuable opportunity to reach and engage your target audience, but it's the quality and relevance of your ad campaigns that will determine your success. In this chapter, we'll explore the key components of creating compelling ads that will capture a viewer's attention, drive clicks, and inspire action.

STRUCTURING YOUR AD CAMPAIGNS

The structure of your ad campaigns plays a crucial role in their effectiveness and efficiency. Without one, ad campaigns can struggle to reach their intended audience, come off as confusing or unprofessional, and waste both your time and your grant.

A well-organized campaign, on the other hand, does the opposite: It allows you to target specific audience segments, tailor your messaging, and optimize your budget allocation. Here are some best practices for structuring your campaigns:

Campaign Hierarchy: Start by creating separate campaigns for each of your nonprofit's main initiatives or programs. This allows you to set specific budgets, targeting options, and performance goals for each campaign.

Ad Groups: Within each campaign, create ad groups that focus on specific themes, topics, or keywords. Ad groups help you organize your ads and landing pages around common ideas, making it easier to deliver relevant content to your audience.

Granularity: Aim for a granular campaign structure, with tightly themed ad groups and targeted keywords. This approach enables you to create highly specific and relevant ads that resonate with your audience's interests and needs.

WRITING COMPELLING AD COPY

Your ad copy is the gateway to engaging your audience and encouraging them to take action. Crafting compelling ad copy is both an art and a science, requiring a deep understanding of your target audience and the ability to communicate your message effectively within the limited space of a search ad. Consider these tips for writing impactful ad copy:

Highlight Your Unique Value Proposition: Clearly communicate what sets your nonprofit apart and why your cause matters. Emphasize the impact and benefits of supporting your mission.

Use Strong, Action-Oriented Language: Encourage users to take specific actions, such as "Donate Now," "Join Our Movement," or "Sign the Petition." Use active verbs and create a sense of urgency to motivate immediate engagement.

Incorporate Keywords: Strategically integrate your targeted keywords into your ad copy, particularly in the headline and description. This helps improve ad relevance and increases the likelihood of your ads appearing for related searches.

Test and Refine: Continuously experiment with different ad variations, testing elements like headlines, descriptions, and calls-to-action. Use A/B testing to identify top-performing variants and optimize your ad copy over time.

UTILIZING AD EXTENSIONS

Ad extensions are additional pieces of information that you can add to your search ads to provide more context, improve visibility, and enhance the user experience. Google Ads offers a variety of ad extensions, each serving a specific purpose. Here are some key extensions to consider:

Sitelink Extensions: Add links to specific pages on your website, such as your donation page, volunteer sign-up form, or program overview. Sitelinks allow users to navigate directly to the most relevant content.

Callout Extensions: Highlight unique selling points or key differentiators of your nonprofit, such as "100% of Donations Go to Programs" or "Rated 4 Stars by Charity Navigator." Callouts provide additional information to entice users to click on your ad.

Call Extensions: Display your nonprofit's phone number directly in your ads, making it easy for users to contact you with questions or to get involved. Call extensions are particularly valuable for driving immediate engagement.

Structured Snippet Extensions: Showcase specific aspects of your nonprofit's work, such as the types of programs you offer or the regions you serve. Structured snippets provide more context and help users understand the scope of your impact.

BEST PRACTICES FOR GOOGLE AD GRANT CAMPAIGNS

To maximize the impact of your Google Ad Grant campaigns, consider these best practices:

Maintain High Quality Scores: Google assigns a Quality Score to each of your keywords, reflecting the relevance and effectiveness of your ads and landing pages. Higher Quality Scores lead to better ad positions and lower costs per click. Focus on creating highly relevant ads and optimizing your landing pages to improve your Quality Scores.

Adhere to Ad Grant Policies: Ensure that your campaigns comply with Google's Ad Grant policies, which include requirements for keyword quality, ad relevance, and landing page experience. Regularly review and update your campaigns to maintain compliance and avoid any disruptions to your ad delivery. We will discuss these policies in more detail in a following chapter.

Monitor and Optimize Performance: Continuously monitor the performance of your campaigns, tracking metrics like click-through rates (CTR), conversion rates, and cost per acquisition (CPA). Use this data to identify areas for improvement and optimize your campaigns accordingly. Regularly adjust your bids, refine your keyword targeting, and experiment with ad variations to enhance performance over time.

CONCLUSION

Creating effective ad campaigns is essential to maximizing the impact of your Google Ad Grant. By structuring your campaigns strategically, writing compelling ad copy, utilizing ad extensions, and following best practices, you can craft ads that resonate with your target audience and drive meaningful engagement.

Remember, effective ad campaigns are an iterative process. It is vital that you continuously test, refine, and optimize your approach based on performance data and user feedback. Stay attuned to your audience's needs and preferences, and adapt your messaging and targeting accordingly.

By mastering the art of creating effective ad campaigns, you'll unlock the full potential of your Google Ad Grant and drive significant results for your nonprofit's mission. In the next chapter, we'll explore the critical role of landing page optimization in converting ad clicks into meaningful actions and support.

Chapter Four

Landing Page Optimization

While crafting compelling ad campaigns is crucial for attracting clicks and driving traffic to your website, the true success of your Google Ad Grant efforts hinges on what happens after the click. This is where landing page optimization comes into play. Your landing pages serve as the critical bridge between your ads and your nonprofit's goals, whether it's encouraging donations, signing up volunteers, or spreading awareness about your cause. In this chapter, we'll dive deep into the art and science of creating high-converting landing pages that maximize the impact of your Ad Grant campaigns.

UNDERSTANDING THE ROLE OF LANDING PAGES

Landing pages are standalone web pages designed to convert visitors into supporters or customers. In the context of Google Ad Grants, your landing pages should be specifically tailored to the intent and expectations of the users who click on your ads. A well-optimized landing page will:

1. Provide a seamless and relevant experience for visitors, aligning with the message and promise of your ads.

2. Clearly communicate your nonprofit's value proposition and the impact of supporting your cause.
3. Motivate visitors to take specific actions, such as making a donation, signing up for a newsletter, or registering for an event.
4. Build trust and credibility through professional design, compelling content, and social proof.

KEY ELEMENTS OF HIGH-CONVERTING LANDING PAGES

To create landing pages that drive conversions, focus on incorporating these essential elements:

Compelling Headline: Your headline should grab attention, reinforce the message of your ad, and communicate the main benefit of taking action.

Clear and Concise Copy: Use straightforward language to convey your value proposition, explain the impact of supporting your cause, and address any potential objections or concerns.

Strong Call-to-Action (CTA): Make your CTA prominent, specific, and action-oriented. Use contrasting colors and engaging button text to encourage clicks.

Visuals and Multimedia: Incorporate relevant images, videos, or infographics to illustrate your message, evoke emotions, and break up text-heavy content.

Social Proof: Include testimonials, success stories, or statistics that demonstrate the credibility and impact of your nonprofit's work.

Mobile-Friendly Design: Ensure your landing pages are optimized for mobile devices, with responsive layouts, fast load times, and easy navigation.

OPTIMIZING LANDING PAGES FOR CONVERSIONS

To maximize the conversion potential of your landing pages, consider these optimization strategies:

Remove Navigation: Eliminate distractions by removing site-wide navigation menus, allowing visitors to focus solely on your landing page content and CTA.

Simplify Forms: Keep your donation or sign-up forms short and simple, asking only for essential information. Use auto-fill and progress indicators to streamline the process.

Optimize for Speed: Ensure your landing pages load quickly, as slow load times can deter visitors and negatively impact conversion rates.

Use A/B Testing: Continuously experiment with different elements of your landing pages, such as headlines, CTAs, and images. Use A/B testing to identify top-performing variants and optimize your pages over time.

Personalize the Experience: Tailor your landing pages to specific audience segments or ad campaigns, using dynamic content and personalized messaging to create a more relevant and engaging experience.

MEASURING AND ANALYZING LANDING PAGE PERFORMANCE

To continually improve your landing pages and maximize conversions, it's crucial to track and analyze key performance metrics. Use tools like Google Analytics and Google Tag Manager to monitor:

Conversion Rate: The percentage of visitors who complete your desired action (e.g., making a donation or signing up for a newsletter).

Bounce Rate: The percentage of visitors who leave your landing page without interacting or taking action.

Time on Page: The average amount of time visitors spend on your landing page, indicating engagement and interest.

Traffic Sources: The channels and campaigns driving traffic to your landing pages, allowing you to identify top-performing sources and allocate your budget accordingly.

Regularly review your landing page analytics and use these insights to inform your optimization efforts. Identify pages with high bounce rates or low conversion rates and prioritize them for improvement. Conduct user testing and gather feedback from visitors to uncover areas of confusion or friction.

Small changes can make a big difference! For example, we work with a client that focuses on getting website visitors to "adopt otters" by becoming recurring donors. These adoptions were infrequent, but then, our team recommended a small change: rearranging the adoption form so that the least expensive option appeared first. This dramatically improved performance, increasing adoptions by 300%, proving that even slight alterations can have a huge impact.

CONCLUSION

Landing page optimization is a critical component of a successful Google Ad Grant strategy. By creating landing pages that align with your ads, communicate your value proposition, and motivate action, you can convert more visitors into engaged supporters and maximize the impact of your grant.

Remember, landing page optimization is an ongoing process. Just like with your keywords and ad campaigns, you should continuously test, analyze, and refine your landing pages based on performance data and user feedback. Stay attuned to best practices and emerging trends in landing page design and optimization.

By mastering the art and science of landing page optimization, you'll unlock the full potential of your Google Ad Grant and drive meaningful results for your nonprofit's cause. In the next chapter, we'll explore the importance of tracking and measuring the performance of your Ad Grant campaigns, providing you with the insights needed to continuously improve and scale your impact.

Chapter Five

Tracking and Measuring Performance

It was Peter Drucker who said, "You can't improve what you don't measure." This is especially relevant when it comes to maximizing the impact of your Google Ad Grant campaigns. By tracking and measuring the performance of your ads and landing pages, you gain invaluable insights into what's working, what's not, and where opportunities for optimization lie. In this chapter, we'll dive deep into the process of setting up conversion tracking, analyzing key metrics, and leveraging data to continuously refine your Ad Grant strategy.

THE IMPORTANCE OF TRACKING AND MEASURING PERFORMANCE

Before we delve into the technical aspects of setting up tracking, let's underscore why it's crucial for your nonprofit's success:

Evaluating Campaign Effectiveness: Tracking performance allows you to assess the effectiveness of your Ad Grant campaigns, identifying which ads, keywords, and landing pages are driving the most conversions and engagement.

Optimizing Budget Allocation: By understanding which campaigns and tactics are yielding the best results, you can optimize your budget allocation, focusing your resources on the highest-performing areas.

Identifying Areas for Improvement: Tracking helps you pinpoint areas of your campaigns that may be underperforming, such as low-converting landing pages or keywords with high bounce rates. This information guides your optimization efforts.

Demonstrating Impact: Measurable data allows you to demonstrate the impact of your Ad Grant efforts to stakeholders, including your team, board members, and supporters.

SETTING UP CONVERSION TRACKING

Conversion tracking is the foundation of measuring your Ad Grant performance. Conversions are the various actions visitors take while on your website, such as making a donation, signing up for a newsletter, or completing a volunteer registration form. We will use two free tools to accomplish this: Google Analytics and Google Tag Manager.

SETTING UP CONVERSION TRACKING IN GOOGLE ANALYTICS 4 (GA4)

To understand how users interact with your website and which actions they're taking that are valuable to your organization, conversion tracking in Google Analytics 4 is essential. This guide will walk you through the process of setting up conversion tracking in GA4, from defining what constitutes a conversion to ensuring the data flows correctly. These instructions are accurate as of the time of writing, though things may have changed slightly in the Google Analytics user interface since then (because they are changing all the time!). Feel free to search YouTube for a video guide with updated instructions if needed, but the steps below will give you the essentials.

Step 1: Set Up Google Analytics 4

Before setting up conversion tracking, ensure that Google Analytics 4 is properly installed on your website. This involves creating a GA4 property and adding the GA4 configuration tag to your website. If you're transitioning from Universal Analytics, you'll need to set up a new GA4 property as it uses a different tracking system.

1. **Create a GA4 Property:**
    a. Go to the Google Analytics website and log in.
    b. Click "Admin" in the lower left corner
    c. In the Account column, make sure your account is selected.
    d. In the Property column, click "+ Create Property" and follow the instructions to create a GA4 property.

2. **Install the GA4 Tracking Code:**
    a. In the GA4 property, go to "Data Streams" under "Data Collection" and add your website.
    b. Follow the instructions to add the provided "Global site tag (gtag.js)" to the header of every webpage or through a tag manager.

Step 2: Define and Set Up Conversions

In GA4, conversions are user interactions that are tracked when they meet criteria you set. These could be form submissions, downloads, sign-ups, or any other key actions relevant to your site.

1. **Identify Your Conversion Events:**
    a. Decide which user actions are valuable as conversions. Common examples include 'form submissions,' 'downloads,' 'sign-ups,' and 'purchases.'

2. **Configure Conversion Events in GA4:**
   a. Navigate to the "Events" section in your GA4 property.
   b. Click "Create Event" to set up new events or modify existing events as conversions. You can use the event naming format that best suits your tracking needs.

3. **Mark Events as Conversions:**
   a. Once you have your events set up, go to "Conversions" in the "Engage" menu.
   b. Click "New Conversion Event" and enter the name of the event you want to track as a conversion. Make sure it exactly matches the event name in GA4.

Step 3: Test Your Conversion Tracking

It's crucial to ensure that the events are being tracked correctly as conversions.

1. **Use Real-Time Reports:**
   a. In GA4, go to "Reports," then "Realtime" to see live data.
   b. Perform the conversion action on your site (e.g., submit a form).
   c. Check if the event shows up in the real-time report as a conversion.

2. **Use DebugView:**
   a. If you have the Google Analytics Debugger installed, you can use "DebugView" under "Configure" in GA4 to test and debug events on your site in real-time.

Step 4: Analyze Conversion Data

Once your conversions are properly set up and data is being collected, you can analyze this data to understand user behavior and optimize your site.

1. **Access Conversion Reports:**
   a. In GA4, navigate to "Reports," then "Engage," and view "Conversions" to analyze detailed reports on your conversion data.

2. **Utilize Analysis Hub:**
   a. For deeper insights, use the "Analysis Hub" under "Explore" where you can perform more complex analysis like cohort analysis, user pathing, and segment overlap.

SETTING UP CONVERSION TRACKING USING GOOGLE TAG MANAGER

Google Tag Manager (GTM) is a powerful tool that simplifies the management of tracking codes and analytics on your website. By using GTM in conjunction with Google Analytics, you can efficiently track specific user interactions such as link clicks or form submissions and mark them as conversions. This guide will cover setting up conversion tracking for two common scenarios: clicks on a specific link and form submissions.

Step 1: Setting Up Google Tag Manager

Before you start tracking conversions, ensure that Google Tag Manager is correctly set up on your website.

1. **Create a GTM Account and Container:**
   a. Visit the Google Tag Manager website and sign in or create an account.

b. Create a new container for your website, selecting "Web" as where you want to use the container.

2. **Install GTM Container Code on Your Website:**

   a. You will receive a GTM container code snippet after creating your container.

   b. Place this code snippet immediately after the opening `<head>` tag and immediately after the opening `<body>` tag on every page of your website.

Step 2: Tracking Link Clicks as Conversions

To track clicks on a specific link (e.g., a donation button), follow these steps:

1. **Create a Trigger for Link Clicks:**

   a. In GTM, go to "Triggers" and click "New."

   b. Name your trigger (e.g., "Donation Link Click").

   c. Set Trigger Type to "Just Links."

   d. Configure the trigger to fire on "Some Link Clicks."

   e. Use conditions to specify which link clicks to track (e.g., Click URL contains '/donate').

2. **Create a Tag to Send Event Data to Google Analytics:**

   a. Go to "Tags" and click "New."

   b. Name your tag (e.g., "Track Donation Link Click").

   c. Set Tag Type to "Google Analytics: GA4 Event."

   d. Configure the tag to send data to your Google Analytics 4 property.

   e. Set the event parameters (e.g., event name: 'donation_click').

f. Associate the tag with the link click trigger you created.

Step 3: Tracking Form Submissions as Conversions

To track form submissions, you can use the following setup:

1. **Create a Trigger for Form Submission:**
    a. In GTM, click "Triggers" then "New."
    b. Name your trigger (e.g., "Form Submission Trigger").
    c. Choose Trigger Type as "Form Submission."
    d. Configure to fire on "Some Forms" if targeting specific forms (e.g., Form ID equals 'signupForm').

2. **Create a Tag to Send Event Data to Google Analytics:**
    a. Go to "Tags" and create a new tag named "Track Form Submission."
    b. Select Tag Type as "Google Analytics: GA4 Event."
    c. Configure to send data such as Event Name: 'form_submission' to your GA4 property.
    d. Link this tag to the form submission trigger.

Step 4: Marking Events as Conversions in Google Analytics

Once you're sending event data to Google Analytics, you need to mark these events as conversions:

1. **Log in to Google Analytics 4 Property:**
    a. Go to "Events" in the left sidebar.
    b. Then, click "Conversions" and "New Conversion Event."

c. Add the event names you've configured in GTM (e.g., 'donation_click', 'form_submission') as conversion events.

Step 5: Testing and Verifying Your Setup

To ensure your tags and triggers are working:

1. **Use GTM Preview Mode:**

    a. Click "Preview" in GTM, enter your website URL, and start the preview session.

    b. Test the interactions (click the specific link, submit the form).

    c. Verify that the correct tags fire when these actions are performed.

2. **Check Real-Time Reports in Google Analytics:**

    a. Navigate to the "Real-time" report in Google Analytics to see if the events are being recorded.

By following these steps, you can effectively track specific user actions as conversions using Google Tag Manager and Google Analytics. This data will provide valuable insights into user behavior and help optimize your website's performance and conversion rates. Be sure to review and update your tags, triggers, and conversion events often, and to keep pace with any changes on your website or in user interactions.

INTEGRATING GOOGLE ADS AND GOOGLE ANALYTICS

Integrating Google Ads with Google Analytics provides a powerful combination for maximizing the effectiveness of your advertising campaigns. By linking these two platforms, you gain deeper insights into how users interact with your ads and website, allowing for more informed decision-making and refined campaign strategies. This guide will walk you through the steps to successfully integrate Google Ads with Google Analytics.

Step 1: Preparing for Integration

Before beginning the integration process, ensure that you have administrative access to both your Google Ads and Google Analytics accounts. This is necessary to make the required changes in each account.

Step 2: Link Google Ads to Google Analytics

1. **Log into Google Analytics:**
   a. Navigate to your Google Analytics account that tracks the data for the website you're advertising with Google Ads.

2. **Access Admin Settings:**
   a. Click on 'Admin' at the lower left corner of your Google Analytics interface.

3. **Link to Google Ads:**
   a. In the middle column labeled 'Property', find 'Google Ads Linking' and click on it.
   b. Click the '+ New link group' button.
   c. You'll see a list of Google Ads accounts. Select the account(s) you want to link to your Google Analytics property.
   d. Click 'Continue' and then provide a title for the link group.
   e. Select the data views in Google Analytics where you want the Google Ads data to be available.
   f. Click 'Link Accounts' to finalize the link.

Step 3: Import Google Analytics Goals into Google Ads

1. **Set Up Conversions in Google Analytics:**

    a. Before importing goals, make sure you have set up goals or e-commerce tracking in your Google Analytics. These will serve as conversion actions in Google Ads.

2. **Import Goals to Google Ads:**

    a. Log into your Google Ads account.

    b. Go to 'Tools & Settings' in the top right, then under 'Measurement', select 'Conversions'.

    c. Click on the '+' button, then select 'Import' from the list of options.

    d. Choose 'Google Analytics' and click 'Continue'.

    e. You will see a list of goals and transactions from Google Analytics. Select the ones you want to track as conversions in Google Ads.

    f. Configure settings such as conversion window and value, then click 'Import and Continue'.

Step 4: Configure Google Analytics to Enhance Google Ads Reporting

1. **Enable Auto-tagging in Google Ads:**

    a. This ensures that Google Analytics can accurately attribute traffic and conversion data to the right Google Ads campaigns.

    b. In Google Ads, go to 'Settings' in the account settings menu.

c. Look for 'Account settings', then find 'Auto-tagging' and ensure it is checked to append a parameter to your URLs automatically.

2. **Adjust Google Analytics Settings:**

   a. To enhance reporting capabilities, enable features such as 'Enhanced Ecommerce' which provides richer data about user interactions on e-commerce sites.

   b. You may also want to explore adjusting the attribution model in Google Analytics to align with how you credit conversions in Google Ads.

ANALYZING KEY PERFORMANCE METRICS

Once you have conversion tracking set up, you can begin analyzing key performance metrics to gain insights into your Ad Grant campaign performance. Here are some essential metrics to monitor:

Conversion Rate: The percentage of ad clicks that result in a desired conversion action. High conversion rates indicate that your ads and landing pages are effectively persuading visitors to take action.

Cost per Conversion: The average amount you spend on Ad Grant clicks for each conversion. Lower costs per conversion suggest that your campaigns are efficiently driving results.

Click-Through Rate (CTR): The percentage of ad impressions that result in clicks. A high CTR indicates that your ads are relevant and compelling to your target audience.

Quality Score: A rating from 1-10 assigned by Google, reflecting the relevance and quality of your ads, keywords, and landing pages. Higher Quality Scores can lead to better ad positions and lower costs per click.

Bounce Rate: The percentage of visitors who leave your website after viewing only one page. High bounce rates may indicate that your landing pages are not meeting visitor expectations or effectively encouraging engagement.

LEVERAGING DATA FOR CONTINUOUS IMPROVEMENT

Tracking and measuring performance is not a one-time event, but rather an ongoing process of learning, iterating, and optimizing. Here's how to use the data you collect to continuously improve your Ad Grant campaigns:

Conduct Regular Audits: Schedule regular audits of your campaigns to review performance data and identify trends, successes, and areas for improvement. Conversion tracking can break for any number of reasons, so you'll want to regularly check to make sure data is still flowing. We have a routine check process that we do for all of our clients to make sure we aren't missing conversions.

Test and Experiment: Use your findings to inform A/B tests and experiments, trying out different ad copy, landing page designs, or targeting strategies to see what drives better results.

Refine Your Approach: Based on your analysis and testing, refine your Ad Grant approach, focusing on the tactics and elements that prove most effective in achieving your goals.

Share Insights: Regularly share performance data and insights with your team and stakeholders to keep everyone informed and aligned on your Ad Grant strategy and progress.

CONCLUSION

Tracking and measuring performance is a vital part of maximizing the impact of your Google Ad Grant campaigns. By setting up conversion tracking, analyzing key metrics, and leveraging data for continuous improvement, you can gain valuable insights into what's working and where to focus your optimization efforts.

Remember, tracking and measuring is an ongoing process that involves experimentation and constant learning. Regularly review your performance data, conduct audits, and use your findings to inform testing and refinement. For the best results, you will need to stay attuned to the best practices and emerging trends in digital marketing analytics.

By mastering the art and science of tracking and measuring performance, you'll unlock the full potential of your Google Ad Grant and make data-driven decisions that maximize your nonprofit's impact. In the next chapter, we'll explore advanced strategies and tips to take your Ad Grant efforts to the next level, from leveraging Google Analytics to experimenting with remarketing and audience targeting.

Chapter Six

Content Marketing

When leveraged tactically, content marketing is a surefire way to foster a long-term relationship with your audience and raise awareness for your nonprofit organization. Content marketing can be particularly useful when paired with the Google Ad Grant. Understanding and defining your content strategy will ensure the content you're producing is valuable, shareable, and successful.

Crafting a comprehensive content marketing strategy for your organization requires an upfront commitment of time and resources. While this can feel daunting at first, it is far more likely to yield long-term gain.

In this chapter, we will define content marketing and its relevance to the Google Ad Grant, explore the different types and benefits, and showcase how you can develop a content marketing strategy for your organization.

UNDERSTANDING CONTENT MARKETING RELATIVE TO THE GOOGLE GRANT

Google's focus is providing a positive user experience, which means offering users the best possible answers to their questions. When your content satisfies a user's questions, they're more likely to click on your ads and spend more time on your site. The more time users spend on your web pages, the greater the chance that Google will reward that page with more organic (free!) traffic.

TYPES OF CONTENT MARKETING

There are several types of content you can use to add depth to your website, whether written or visual. To make the most of content marketing, it's vital to understand the different types of content you can employ and to choose the best option for your strategy.

Blogging: Blogging can improve search engine optimization (SEO) for a nonprofit organization's website, making it easier for people to find them online.

Social Media: Nonprofit organizations can use social media platforms like Facebook, Instagram, and Linkedin to connect and share content with a broader audience.

Email Marketing: Email marketing enables nonprofit organizations to stay in touch with their supporters, share news and updates, and encourage donations. Its high return on investment makes it a cost-effective fundraising tool.

Video Marketing: Nonprofit organizations can use video marketing to share their impact stories, educate their audience about their cause, and inspire action. Video marketing is on an upswing, with short-form videos generating the highest ROI.

Infographics: Using infographics is an excellent way for nonprofit organizations to present their impact data and simplify complex information in a format that is both visually appealing and easy-to-understand. Infographics are easily shared and attention-grabbing, which can help generate interest in and broaden the reach of your organization's message.

THE BENEFITS OF CONTENT MARKETING

Improves Ad Relevance: Creating high-quality and informative content that aligns with your organization's mission improves the relevance of your Google Grant ads. As a result, this can lead to higher click-through rates (CTR) and more conversions. According to Google, ad relevance is a critical factor in determining Ad Rank, which is the position of your ad on the search page results.

Increases Website Traffic: Promoting your content through various channels like social media, email marketing, and search engine optimization (SEO) can drive more traffic to your organization's website. High levels of relevant traffic help with your overall Google Ranking, which helps increase your Google Ad Grant clicks and bolster your online presence.

Builds Trust and Authority: Consistently creating and sharing valuable content reinforces your nonprofit organization as a thought leader in your industry. This can help you build trust with potential donors, volunteers, and other stakeholders and drive more support for your cause. Grant-funded ads help you amass the greatest number of potential supporters with your content.

Supports SEO Efforts: Incorporating relevant keywords and topics into your content supports your organization's SEO efforts. As a result, you can rank higher in both organic search results *and* Google Ad rankings, and drive more traffic to your site over time.

Developing Your Content Marketing Strategy

Step 1: Determine Your Purpose

First, you need to identify the intended purpose of your content marketing strategy and define it in clear and concrete terms. Knowing the "why" will help you specify your target audience and the best ways to meet your goals, creating a strong foundation for your content strategy.

Step 2: Understand Your Audience

The key to creating compelling content is understanding what your audience is looking for and how best to educate them on your mission. To do this, dive into your data: find the demographic most responsive to your cause and what they are interested in learning about your organization. You can do this with surveys, focus groups, site analytics, or other research methods.

Once you've established your audience and their focus, create a blueprint for future content based on these insights. Your goals should be to provide helpful information about the issue at hand and make sure it leads to engagement opportunities (newsletter signups, donations and volunteer events).

The engagement your content promotes should go hand-in-hand with the priorities of your content marketing strategy.

Step 3: Define Key Performance Metrics

Defining your metrics ahead of time is the only way to know if you've reached them once you publish your content. Frequently gauging the status of these metrics and reevaluating the success of your content strategy will allow you to make necessary tweaks over time. Your metrics for each form of content should align with one another.

Step 4: Examine Your Existing Content

Looking at your existing content marketing efforts is a critical step to ensure you're setting realistic goals for your strategy.

You can begin the process by answering these questions:

- What types of content are we publishing?
- Where are those pieces being published (e.g. your website or blog, an email newsletter, or on social media)?

- How much time and money have we spent creating this type of content over the last year?

A thorough assessment of your content in all its forms and across all of your platforms is a great way to learn what is and isn't working. It will also help you determine where you can improve your content and its delivery.

Step 5: Ensure Your Content Answers Questions

It's crucial that your content is able to articulate your intended message and answers questions posed by your audience. You want to meet consumers' informational and resource-related needs in a way that illustrates your understanding of their requisites and appreciation of their support.

Step 6: Identify Content Distribution Channels

It's effective to know which channels will optimize reader engagement with your content. You can identify short-term and long-term strategies by using channel metrics. These strategies should include more than one channel (known as "omnichannel strategies" in the marketing world) and incorporate both online and offline channels.

Step 7: Develop a Content Calendar

Based on your thorough audit of existing content and goals, put together a content production plan (also called an editorial calendar). This calendar should include a process to determine content type, who will create your content, how the content should be distributed, and task deadlines.

While following your content calendar will go a long way toward captivating new users, it doesn't have to be cast in stone. Plans change, so you must also be flexible and enable your organization to switch gears when necessary.

Writing consistently high-quality content can be very difficult to do. We have a writing team producing dozens of SEO and Google Grant optimized in-depth articles for our clients each month, and would love to help you do the same. Feel free to reach out to us at hello@nonprofitmegaphone.com for more details.

CONCLUSION

Content marketing is a valuable and economical tool for nonprofit organizations to advance their mission. Investing time and energy into developing a content marketing strategy can help you take full advantage of the many benefits content marketing offers.

It's a simple formula: the easier it is to find you online, the more likely people are to engage with your organization and ultimately donate or volunteer.

Chapter Seven

Maintaining Compliance and Avoiding Common Mistakes

Introduction

To maintain access to the $10,000 monthly advertising budget, all nonprofits must comply with the Google Ad Grant program's rules. This chapter explores the key compliance requirements and provides guidance on how to best adhere to Google's policies to ensure your nonprofit continues to benefit from this valuable resource.

UNDERSTANDING GOOGLE AD GRANT POLICIES

The Google Ad Grant program has specific policies designed to ensure that the ads run by nonprofits are relevant, effective, and aligned with the goals of the program. Understanding these policies is the first step toward maintaining compliance.

1. **Mission-Based Campaigns:**
   - Your ads and keywords must be closely related to your nonprofit's mission.
   - Ads promoting products or services unrelated to your nonprofit are not allowed.

2. **Website Ownership and Quality:**
   - You must own the domain of the website linked in your ads.
   - The website should have substantial content, be easy to navigate, and provide a good user experience.

3. **Active Account Management:**
   - You must log into your Google Ads account at least once a month and make at least one change to your account every 90 days to show that the account is actively managed.

4. **Ad Strategies and Structures:**
   - Google Ads should have proper ad groups structure, with each ad group targeting a set of closely related keywords.
   - Single-word keywords are generally not permitted (with some exceptions), and overly generic keywords must be avoided.

5. **Tracking and Reporting:**
   - Conversion tracking must be set up to measure the effectiveness of your ads.
   - This helps demonstrate that the ad grant is contributing to your nonprofit's goals.

COMMON COMPLIANCE ISSUES AND SOLUTIONS

Understanding common compliance pitfalls can help prevent unintentional violations that could lead to account suspension.

1. **Problem: Ineffective Keyword Choices**
   - Solution: Regularly review and refine your keyword lists. Remove underperforming or irrelevant keywords that do not contribute to your goals.

2. **Problem: Low-Quality Ads**
   - Solution: Ensure that ad copy is compelling, directly related to the keywords, and includes a clear call-to-action. Test different versions of your ads to find the most effective messaging.

3. **Problem: Lack of Optimization**
   - Solution: Use the data from Google Analytics and Google Ads to optimize your campaigns continually. Focus on improving your Quality Score by enhancing the relevancy of your ads and landing pages.

4. **Problem: Non-Functional Website**
   - Solution: Regularly check your website for broken links, outdated content, and poor navigation. Ensure that the landing pages linked from your ads are fully functional and provide valuable content.

BEST PRACTICES FOR ENSURING COMPLIANCE

Adopting these best practices for account management will not only help maintain compliance, but also enhance the overall efficiency of your campaigns.

1. **Regular Account Reviews:**
   - Schedule weekly reviews of your Google Ads account to check for any issues that might affect compliance.

2. **Utilize Google's Resources:**
   - Google provides several resources and tools to help nonprofits manage their Ad Grants effectively. Make use of Google's Ad Grants Help Center and participate in forums and webinars.

3. **Document Changes and Performance:**
   - Keep records of changes made in your account and monitor how these changes affect your campaign performance. This documentation can be invaluable for troubleshooting issues and proving active management in case of an audit.

If you have run into Google Grant compliance issues or even had your account suspended, don't hesitate to reach out. We are happy to help you get reactivated and ensure that you always stay in compliance going forward.

CONCLUSION

Maintaining compliance with the Google Ad Grant program is crucial if you want to continue benefiting from the free advertising budget. By understanding and adhering to Google's policies, regularly reviewing and optimizing your account, and staying informed about best practices, your nonprofit can effectively use the Google Ad Grant to reach more people, increase engagement, and further your mission.

Chapter Eight

The Impact of Using a Google Ad Grants Certified Professional Agency

Introduction

Navigating the complexities of Google Ad Grants can be challenging, especially for nonprofits that may not have dedicated marketing expertise. This is where Google Ad Grants Certified Professional agencies come into play. This chapter explores the benefits of partnering with a certified agency, the services they provide, and the overall impact on a nonprofit's digital marketing efforts.

UNDERSTANDING GOOGLE AD GRANTS CERTIFIED PROFESSIONAL AGENCIES

A Google Ad Grants Certified Professional Agency is an organization recognized by Google for having expert knowledge in managing Google Ad Grants accounts. These agencies not only understand the technical aspects of Google Ads but also have a proven track record of helping nonprofits maximize the value of their grants.

BENEFITS OF PARTNERING WITH A CERTIFIED AGENCY

1. **Expertise and Experience:**
   - Certified agencies have a deep understanding of both Google Ads and the specific needs of nonprofits. They bring years of experience and insights from working with multiple clients, which can significantly improve the effectiveness of your campaigns.

2. **Compliance and Best Practices:**
   - Staying compliant with Google's policies is crucial for maintaining access to Ad Grants. Certified professionals are up-to-date with the latest compliance requirements and can manage your account to avoid pitfalls that might lead to suspension.

3. **Strategic Campaign Management:**
   - Beyond basic management, certified agencies offer strategic planning tailored to your nonprofit's goals. Whether it's increasing donations, recruiting volunteers, or raising awareness, they structure campaigns to achieve specific objectives.

4. **Advanced Reporting and Analytics:**
   - These agencies employ sophisticated tools and techniques for tracking and analyzing the performance of ad campaigns. This data-driven approach enables continuous optimization and clearer demonstration of ROI.

IMPACT ON NONPROFIT ORGANIZATIONS

1. **Increased Visibility and Reach:**
   - By optimizing ad campaigns, certified professionals can significantly increase the visibility of your nonprofit in search results, broadening your reach and attracting more potential supporters.

2. **Higher Engagement and Conversion Rates:**
   - Expert campaign management ensures that your ads are relevant and engaging, leading to higher click-through and conversion rates. This means more effective use of the Ad Grant budget, with more visitors taking desired actions on your website.

3. **Resource Efficiency:**
   - Outsourcing Ad Grants management to a certified agency allows your staff to focus on core organizational tasks. This not only saves time but also ensures that your digital marketing efforts are handled by experts, reducing the likelihood of costly errors.

4. **Scalability:**
   - As your organization grows, a certified agency can adjust and scale your advertising strategies to meet changing needs and opportunities, guaranteeing that your digital presence evolves in line with your goals.

CHOOSING THE RIGHT CERTIFIED AGENCY

When selecting a certified agency, consider the following:

- Reputation and Reviews: Look for agencies with positive testimonials and case studies.

- **Alignment with Your Mission:** Choose an agency that understands and is enthusiastic about your cause.
- **Transparency and Communication:** Ensure they offer clear reporting and maintain open lines of communication.
- **Cost:** Evaluate their fees relative to the potential ROI they offer. Consider the ROI not only from direct ad performance, but also from cost savings, avoidance of issues or errors and peace of mind.

If you are open to working with a partner to manage the Google Grant for you, we at Nonprofit Megaphone (nonprofitmegaphone.com) would love to explore that with you! We are honored to manage more Google Ad Grants than anyone in the world, and would be thrilled to put that experience to work for you and your organization.

We hope this short book has given you a helpful overview of what the Google Grant program is, how it works, and what pitfalls to avoid. In the next section, we have included nearly 50 case studies of how our own clients have used the Google Grant very effectively to help advance their missions. Let these case studies inspire you - your organization can have these kinds of results too!

Case Studies

This Case Studies section has been organized by the type of nonprofit. You are encouraged to flip to the category that best describes your own organization to see the examples that might be most relevant to you.

- The categories are:
- Animals
- Arts & Culture
- Civil & Social
- Education
- Environmental
- Health
- Human & Civil Rights
- Human Services
- Faith & Religion
- Sports & Athletics
- Youth

Without further ado: let's jump into the case studies!

ANIMAL NONPROFIT CASE STUDIES

Chattanooga Zoo: Inspiring Conservation

- **4,500+ New Website Visitors per Day**
- **60+ Avg. Monthly Phone Calls Generated from Ads**
- **12% Average Click Through Rate**

The Chattanooga Zoo creates meaningful interactions between people and wildlife through immersive experiences. The second part of the zoo's mission statement refers to being a premier destination for locals and tourists, which requires significant exposure.

To achieve this exposure, Chattanooga Zoo partnered with Nonprofit Megaphone to advertise to individuals and families looking for family attractions, zoos, or fun activities in their geographic area. In addition, when searchers see ads on their mobile devices they are given a one-click option to call the Zoo, which is generating roughly dozens of inbound calls per month. Running effective campaigns has significantly increased exposure for the Zoo, and is helping the organization fulfill multiple aspects of its mission.

> *"Since working with Nonprofit Megaphone, the Chattanooga Zoo has continuously seen new website visitors with a click-through rate that is over two times the industry average. Working with them is great and the results easily show the success in our partnership."*
>
> — Hannah Hammon, Director of Marketing, Membership & Communication: Chattanooga Zoo

Kennel to Couch: Saving Pit Bulls, One Wet Nose At A Time

- **5,900+ New People Engaging with the Website Monthly**
- **9.76% Click Through Rate on Ads**
- **45+ Conversions to Sponsor a Pit Bull in a Month**

Kennel to Couch is teaming up with shelters and community partners to provide the support needed to encourage adoption for "at risk" Pit Bulls as nearly half a million Pit Bulls are euthanized in animal shelters every year. Kennel To Couch was founded by Thomas Bohne. Thomas became familiar with Pit Bulls and their adverse publicity when he and his family rescued "Rocky" and discovered the love and loyalty that a Pit Bull offers their families, but are so misunderstood by the media and the public.

When Rocky suddenly passed away in 2018, the family was devastated. In Rocky's memory, Kennel to Couch was born, and it's been an incredible journey for this wonderful organization. They partnered with the Humane Society of Hartford County, MD with the mission of helping their longest-tenured Pit bull get adopted. Within two months, he was adopted, and since that time, seven Pit Bulls have been adopted!

> *"We had 80 visitors to our website in the month before we started, and since working with NPM, we now have between 4,500 to 5,000 per month."*
>
> — *Thomas Bohne*

Partnering with animal organizations is one of NPM's specialties, and it was easy to get behind Kennel to Couch's mission to manage their Google Ads Grant. The results are really quite impressive! Last month, Kennel to Couch maintained a 9.76% click-through-rate. That is twice the rate that that Grant requires. They also have over 5,900 new individuals visit their website monthly. NPM is excited to provide expert Google Ad management for Kennel to Couch and to further their mission to rescue abandoned or abused Pit Bulls.

Educated Canines Assisting with Disabilities: Providing Mobility & Independence

- **170+ People Watching ECAD's Live Cam Feed**
- **7.44% Click Through Rate on Ads**
- **2,084 New Website Visitors in a Month**

Educated Canines Assisting with Disabilities (ECAD) has a special mission – to educate and place service dogs with people with disabilities to help them lead lives with more independence and mobility. With such a fantastic mission, they are transforming the lives of people with all kinds of disabilities, including Multiple Sclerosis, Parkinson's Disease, Sleep Apnea, Cerebral Palsy, spinal cord injuries, PTSD, and so much more.

Their Core Programs provide help to specific groups of people. Open Doors provides service dogs and facility dogs for people with disabilities. The Canine Magic Program is unique because it provides specially educated service dogs to assist children with autism. Project HEAL was formed to help veteran's in need who have Post Traumatic Stress Disorder or Traumatic Brain Injury.

Partnering with Nonprofit Megaphone, ECAD has seen tremendous success with its Google Ad campaigns. While the country began to shelter in place, ECAD and NPM partnered to boost their campaigns for their Live Puppy Cam as well as their Live Training Classes, and the results were amazing! At the height of the shut-down, with the help of Google Ads, ECAD saw over 380 different users checking out their live cam feed. Now that most things have opened up, they are still realizing over 150+ live cam users on a monthly basis and maintaining a solid click-through-rate of 7.44%.

> *NPM has "helped me to better understand what to expect from Google Ads . . . and is also great at helping me to come up with new and exciting things to talk about on the blog. It doesn't feel like a vendor/ organization relationship, it feels more like they are just part of our team and work remotely."*
>
> — Carrie Picard, Director of Marketing & Communication

In addition to managing the Google Ads Grant, ECAD has also partnered with NPM to boost their website traffic with the SEO Content Add-On and SEO Optimization Add-On. NPM creates new blog articles and performs website optimizations regularly for ECAD, helping even more people to hear about their mission and the impact that ECAD-trained service dogs make possible.

ACC of NYC: Helping Homeless Pets

- **4,000+ New People Engaging with the Website Monthly**
- **13.99% Click Through Rate on Ads**
- **278 Conversions from Ads**

Animal Care Centers (ACC) of NYC works to find loving homes for homeless and abandoned pets and end animal homelessness across all of New York City. The nonprofit partners with more than 200 dedicated animal placement organizations and collaborates directly with the public, working tirelessly to find a loving place for all animals in their care.

While vision is important, the results are even more so… and ACC of NYC is doing a great job! In any given month, the organization receives hundreds or thousands of dogs and cats that are brought in from the public, surrendered, or seized in the five boroughs of New York City. ACC of NYC then gets to work, rehoming or returning these pets to their owners or transferring them to organizations within their community or coalition. Without the fantastic work of the ACC of NYC, most of these pets would remain homeless and in real danger.

Making the decision to partner with Nonprofit Megaphone has yielded amazing results in their online presence and website traffic, furthering the ability to take care of these precious animals. Within their first 30 days of working with NPM, the number of new people visiting their website from the Google Ad Grant increased by 57%, jumping to more than 3,800 visitors. Additionally, they also doubled their conversions in their first month with NPM managing their Google Ads, with a total of 588 conversions. Of particular note, ACC of NYC reports that many of the people interested in adopting homeless pets are finding the organization through Google Ads, more so in fact, than through any other channel!

NPM & Animal Care Centers of NYC have been partnering together for over two years now, and they continue to see amazing results, keeping a steady click-through rate at almost 14%! NPM is not only excited to see numbers like this, but proud to partner with such great organizations as ACC of NYC and to help them further their cause to end animal homelessness in New York City.

The Grey Muzzle Organization: Saving Senior Dogs

- **4,400+ New People Engaging with the Grey Muzzle Website per Month**
- **8.57% Click Through Rate on Ads**
- **15+ People Signing Up for Email Lists or Contact Forms per Month**

The Grey Muzzle Organization (greymuzzle.org) fights to create a world where no old dog dies alone and afraid.

The nonprofit is one of only a handful of rescue groups in the United States dedicated to helping senior dogs find homes and loving families when they are abandoned. Many times, when extra care is required for the health of a senior dog, these animals are left at shelters or abandoned to homelessness. The Grey Muzzle exists to aid animal welfare organizations in their ability to provide quality care and find homes for these older dogs.

One of the many ways that The Grey Muzzle comes alongside these organizations is by raising money that can be distributed to rescue groups and animal welfare organizations. The Grey Muzzle also provides an accountability system for organizations and offers programs to help them improve their care for these often forgotten dogs.

Partnering with Nonprofit Megaphone to use the Google Ad Grant, The Grey Muzzle is reaching more and more people and more animal rescue organizations with its mission to help senior dogs find homes or the care they need. The results have been outstanding. They have seen over 4,400 new people coming to their website each month from ads, with 15+ people filling out forms or signing up for email lists. Together we can help protect senior dogs, one click at a time.

Yavapai Humane Society: Protecting Companion Animals

- **3,000+ New Website Visitors Monthly**
- **9% Average Click Through Rate**
- **15 Calls from Ads**

Yavapai Humane Society is committed to ensuring that every companion animal in the Prescott, Arizona community has a great home and is well cared for during its lifetime. Every year, the Yavapai Humane Society saves over 2,500 animals and partners with animal control agencies and pet owners to help return lost or homeless animals to their owners or find loving homes for them.

The Yavapai Humane Society offers a wide variety of services, including spay/neuter, a walk-in clinic, dog licensing, and even a pet guardianship program. They also provide animal welfare programs such as their animal enrichment program. This program is designed to ensure a better adoption for homeless pets by retraining them in valuable skills and giving them love and attention.

Nonprofit Megaphone has enjoyed the opportunity of managing the Google Ad Grant for Yavapai Humane Society for over three years. During that time, they have seen over 140,000 new visitors to their website and have maintained a click-through-rate of 9%. We continue to be thrilled and thankful to have the opportunity to partner with Yavapai Humane Society.

ARTS & CULTURE NONPROFIT CASE STUDIES

Omaha Symphony: Driving Ticket Sales

- **3,100+ New Website Visitors Monthly**
- **7.75% Click Through Rate**
- **35,000+ Average Monthly Impressions**

As the largest performing arts organization in Nebraska, the Omaha Symphony has been a keystone institution in its community for over 90 years. The Symphony is committed to enriching lives through the power of live orchestral music, and this mission requires reaching an increasingly broad audience to share that experience. The Omaha Symphony partners with Nonprofit Megaphone in using the Google Ad Grant to reach a very targeted set of individuals who display interest in music and call them to action to attend a performance.

Google Ads allows the Omaha Symphony to reach the public "where they are." Many visitors are in the initial stages of their research, having searched keywords such as "upcoming concerts" or "concerts near me." These individuals may not be aware of the Symphony prior to searching, but they are quickly introduced through very high performing ads. Even in the midst of COVID-19, their account continues to perform well. In October 2021, they received more than 3,100 new visitors to their website and had over 40,000 impressions.

Columbus Symphony: We Are Here For YOU

- **3,100+% New Website Visitors Monthly**
- **14.86% Click Through Rate on Ads**
- **21,400+ Average Monthly Impressions**

The Columbus Symphony, founded in 1951 and in its 70th year, is rolling out a 3-year initiative called "We are Here For YOU," a plan that is focusing on the extraordinary and meaningful service to the central Ohio community. During their three-year focus, they will be focusing on reaching the entire population groups of the residents of Columbus and the surrounding areas, including students, diverse populations, famlies, businesses, rural communities, individual with disabilities, and so many more!

Partnering with Nonprofit Megaphone to manage their Google Ads has brought some amazing results! Thanks to the detailed and focused grant management, the Columbus Symphony is maintaining an average click-through-rate of 14.86%. The number of impressions per month is over 21,000, and they are seeing over 3,000 new visitors to their website monthly. NPM loves to see results like these and enjoys playing a small role in helping nonprofits make a difference in their communities.

Greater Boston Stage Company: The Friendliest Professional Theatre in Boston!

- **1,200+ New People Engaging with the Website Monthly**
- **9.75% Click Through Rate on Ads**
- **70+ Average New Ticket Sales From Ads**

The Greater Boston Stage Company provides a dynamic theatre experience for audiences beyond the boundaries of Boston, featuring world and regional premieres as well as fresh interpretations of traditional work. Greater Boston Stage Company produces 6-7 shows each year and works with the highest caliber of professional actors, directors, and designers, keeping the art of professional theatre thriving.

The vision of Greater Boston Stage Company is to seek to strengthen community in the Boston area by encouraging first-time and seasoned audiences to experience the excitement of live theatre as well as educating up and coming young actors. Their education program, The Young Company, provides year-round training and performance opportunities to students in grades 1-12, and these students have an opportunity to work alongside and learn from the professional company.

Nonprofit Megaphone is thrilled to partner with Great Boston Stage Company to manage their Google Ads and bring wonderful, live theatre experiences to their community. Last quarter, over 1,200 people visited their website and they enjoyed a click-through-rate of 9.75%. It's even more exciting to see that over 100 people bought tickets as a direct result of the Google Ads last month!

Des Moines Symphony: Enriching, Educating & Inspiring

- **120+ Total Conversions**
- **1,900+ New Website Visitors**
- **30,000+ Average Monthly Impressions**

The Des Moines Symphony is Central Iowa's largest professional performing arts organization. Providing quality orchestral music to the Des Moines and surrounding areas for over 81 years, the Des Moines Symphony has become one of the country's outstanding regional orchestras.

While the Symphony provides a range of concerts every year, including a regular series of Masterworks, Pops, Family, and Education Concerts, what many people might not know is they are one of only four American orchestras to sponsor an Academy of Music. This has become core to the mission of the Des Moines Symphony, providing education and opportunities to the future performers of America.

The Google Ad Grant and partnership with Nonprofit Megaphone is a vital part of their marketing strategy. Nonprofit Megaphone facilitated the awareness of their virtual content during the Covid-19 pandemic and continued to provide expert ads during the reopening for live concerts and educational opportunities. They continue to see over 2,000 visitors to their website daily as well as over 100 conversions each month. NPM is excited to partner with such a great community organization!

CIVIC & SOCIAL NONPROFIT CASE STUDIES

The Ladies Talkshow with Leah: Saving & Enriching Marriages

- **6,000+ New People Engaging with the Website Monthly**
- **7.97% Click Through Rate on Ads**
- **75,800+ Average Monthly Impressions**

The Ladies Talkshow hosts a live show every week with the sole purpose of enriching and saving marriages. Founder and host, Leah Richeimer, is a relationship expert and author who is passionate about relationships that are not only fulfilling, but continually growing and improving.

Donating her time and effort to this cause, she conducts a weekly video show that can be viewed live or watched at a time that is more convenient for her viewers. These weekly shows, including titles like "A Wife's Power During Lockdown" and "Comedy Hour: Anger Management," provide valuable encouragement for women to continue to put work into their marriage every day.

> *"I don't know where we would be without NPM. Our clicks are through the roof now. We were getting a few hundred hits on our website a month, and now we're getting that in a single day."*
>
> *— Leah Richeimer*

Since partnering with NPM, The Ladies Talkshow has seen amazing results from expert management of their Google Ad Grant. In the last month, over 75,870 people have seen their ads, and over 6,000 of those visited their website. These numbers have resulted in a click-through-rate of 7.97%. We are thrilled to work alongside The Ladies Talkshow and are looking forward to helping them advance their mission throughout our partnership.

Communities Foundation of Texas: Where Giving Thrives, Communities Thrive

- **3,800+ New People Engaging with the Website Monthly**
- **7.75% Click Through Rate on Ads**
- **36,000+ New People Engaging with the Website Yearly**

Communities Foundation of Texas is one of 700 foundations in the world whose focus is on improving the quality of life for their region. Working alongside donors, nonprofits, businesses, and civic leaders, they strive everyday to build thriving communities for the great state of Texas.

CFT makes it their mission to support their caring donors by providing exemplary service, wise stewardship, and trusted partnerships. Some examples of the amazing work that CFT is doing include making grants to support community issues in North Texas, encouraging individuals, families, and businesses, being careful stewards of $1.1 billion in assets across more than 1,000 charitable funds, and educating the community on pressing needs.

At Nonprofit Megaphone, we consider it an honor to come alongside CFT and strive to make their online presence known by managing their Google Ads. It's been exciting to see their online presence grow as a result of their Google Ads. They have a successful click-through-rate at 7.75%, and the amount of traffic to their website has seen tremendous growth since we started working with them in 2018, growing from 970 people visiting their website each month to over 3,000 people!

Rotary International: Inspiring People of Action

- **80k+ New Website Visitors from the Google Grant**
- **1,169 Visitors Taking Action to Become Rotary Members**
- **795k+ Ad Impressions for Re-Inspired Rotary Brand Globally**

Rotary is where neighbors, friends, and problem-solvers share ideas, join leaders, and take action to create lasting change: across the globe, in our communities, and in ourselves.

Solving real problems takes real commitment and vision. For more than 110 years, Rotary's people of action have used their passion, energy, and intelligence to take action on sustainable projects. From literacy and peace to water and health, we are always working to better our world, and we stay committed to the end.

Rotary members believe that we have a shared responsibility to take action on our world's most persistent issues. Our 35,000+ clubs work together to:

- Promote peace
- Fight disease
- Provide clean water, sanitation, and hygiene
- Save mothers and children
- Support education
- Grow local economies

Since coming on board with Nonprofit Megaphone, Rotary has seen:

- 80,128 people have clicked on their ads.
- 795,985 people have seen their ads.
- Their CTR is 10.07%.
- We have spent $46,504 of the Grant for them.
- They have received 114 calls from ads.

- 1,169 people have filled out the membership form and become a Rotary member after clicking on an ad.

EDUCATION NONPROFIT CASE STUDIES

Kiwanis: Serving the Children of the World

- **3,700+ New Website Visitors Monthly**
- **8.79% Click Through Rate on Ads**
- **296 People Finding Local Clubs**

Kiwanis International is a global community of clubs, members, and partners focused on improving the lives of children and young people. With more than 500,000 members from all over the world, Kiwanis provides the opportunity for members to serve their communities by fighting hunger, improving literacy, and offering guidance.

Each year, Kiwanis members host over 150,000 service projects and complete more than 19 million service hours. Their desire to help kids grow and succeed remains at the forefront of all that they do. Many clubs sponsor a Kiwanis family club – K-Kids for primary school children; Builders Clubs for adolescents; Key Clubs for teens; Circle K clubs for university students and Aktion Clubs for adults living with disabilities.

Utilizing the Google Ad Grant has given Kiwanis a tremendous opportunity to spread the word about their fantastic organization! In the last month, their ads were shown more than 42,500 times which resulted in over 3,743 visits to their website and a CTR of 8.79%. In addition, 296 people showed interest in finding a club near them. NPM is excited to help bring more good to the world through organizations like Kiwanis to manage their Google Ad Grant.

International School Services: Building a Global Educational Community

- **5,300+ New People Engaging with the Website Monthly**
- **8.16% Click Through Rate on Ads**
- **65,000+ Average Monthly Impressions**

International Schools Services began over 60 years ago with the mission to help international schools and educators develop students into thoughtful, imaginative global leaders. Today, they are one of the world's leading nonprofit organizations devoted to supporting the global education community.

Their team of 60+ people has extensive experience in all aspects of international education, including school leadership, school finances and accounting, curriculum development, teaching and learning, and more. Currently, ISS works with more than 500 international schools and thousands of educators each year.

"Working with Nonprofit Megaphone has given us new possibilities to impact more lives with our mission. Having custom-made Google Ads has improved our outreach capabilities in ways that we could not have otherwise accomplished. Whatever comes up, they have it taken care of. We can relax knowing they're creating and monitoring ads that are giving us the best possible outcomes. It is because of that that ISS could not think of working with another organization."

— Keith Fenner, Digital Specialist

Through their partnership with Nonprofit Megaphone, ISS has been able to further its mission through well-positioned and high-performing ads. The results of the creative Google Ad Management have been impressive! During the last month, they had over 65,000 impressions, resulting in 5,309 new visitors to their website! Their average click-through-rate has remained steady around 8.16% throughout the challenges of the Covid-19 pandemic. The Grant Management team at NPM is excited to continue creating and monitoring their ads to give ISS the best possible outcomes.

National Council of Nonprofits: Strengthening Nonprofits

- **6,000+ Monthly New Visitors from Ads**
- **7.40% Average Click Through Rate**
- **150 Monthly Newsletter Submissions**

National Council of Nonprofits is the largest network of nonprofits in the country. Their mission is to keep nonprofits informed and empowered to create a positive public policy environment that best supports nonprofits in their missions. They can do this by identifying emerging trends, sharing proven practices, and promoting solutions that benefit charitable nonprofits and the communities they share.

With so many policies and changes that occur within the nonprofit sector, the National Council of Nonprofits keeps their focus on the health and well-being of all nonprofits, and especially the small and mid-sized charities in local communities. They also help to integrate public policy so that they can identify patterns, opportunities, or even threats to charitable nonprofits. Through e-newsletters, website information, national webinars and conference calls, or Special Reports, they supply timely information to nonprofits throughout the U.S.

NPM is celebrating its two-year anniversary of our partnership with National Council of Nonprofits! We are thrilled to help all nonprofits by providing expert Google Ad Grant management to this fantastic organization! During the last month, more than 5,900 people visited their website for the first time, and their ads were shown over 88,000 times. Conversions are also a great sign of success, and last month, they had 150 newsletter submissions! These results are a fantastic example of how NPM's attention to detail and our client's needs result in excellent Google Ads management, and we look forward to another great year working with National Council of Nonprofits!

Las Vegas-Clark County Library District: Something For Everyone

- **4,100+ New People Engaging with the Website Monthly**
- **13.60% Click Through Rate on Ads**
- **73 Total Conversions**

Las Vegas-Clark County Library District seeks to provide social, economic, and educational materials to improve the well-being of its community. Serving over 1.6 million people in the city of Las Vegas, they are committed to building communities of people who can come together to pursue their individual and group aspirations.

LVCCLD is more than your usual library. Not only do they loan books and promote learning through reading, but they also have performing arts theaters that rival entertainment offered by local casinos. Additionally, they have free art galleries. In fact, one of the selling points for partnering with NPM was the ability to advertise their art galleries and the special events they host. Although some of these services have been delayed due to COVID-19, LVCCLD remains steadfast in its commitment to provide opportunities for the communities they serve while maintaining social distancing. All local libraries are fully reopened and other in-demand services such as One-Stop Career services, art gallery exhibitions, Safe Place services for youth in crisis, and adult literacy and education courses are available.

Nonprofit Megaphone is incredibly excited to partner with LVCCLD to manage their Google Ad Grant. The results in just a few months are amazing! During their first month, their ads received more than 3,000 impressions, 500 of which were new website visitors. And the ongoing results are even more incredible! In September 2021, their Google Ad presence continued to increase, resulting in over 30,000 impressions and over 4,100 clicks! We look forward to helping LVCCLD further advance their mission to strengthen its communities through the services they offer.

Human Assistance & Development International: Assisting in the Development of Humankind

- **58,900+ Monthly New Visitors from Ads**
- **15.62% Click Through Rate on Ads**
- **377,556 Impressions From Ads**

Human Assistance & Development International (HADI) helps thousands of people around the world to work for socio-economic, educational, and scientific development worldwide without any boundaries as to race, creed, or color. Amazingly, what started in 1991 as a way to give back to society for their own success after they immigrated to the United States, the founders of the organization have made it their goal to dedicate knowledge, talent and time for the long-term development of people worldwide.

Fast-forward almost 20 years, and HADI has a long list of accomplishments, including launching the first Islamic Radio channel online with over 50,000 visitors, establishing the Center for Languages, Arts & Societes of SilkRoad (CLASSRoad), which improves cross-cultural understanding across and between East and West in today's world, as well as completing BRIGHT (Balance Resilience Integrity Goodness Harmony Tolerance) Teacher Training pilot program for California Public Schools. They also manage IslamiCity. org, which provides a non-sectarian, comprehensive and holistic view of Islam and Muslims. Its goal is to cultivate peace, inspire action, explore positive solutions and encourage purposeful living through the universal teachings of Islam.

The Google Ad Grant program has been a catalyst for HADI to get the word out about their amazing organization. NPM is excited to come alongside them to manage their Google Ads, producing outstanding results! In the last 30 days, their click-through-rate has remained at an average 15.62%, well above Google's requirement of 5%. Even more impressive is that their ads have been seen over 377,500 times with 58,900 new people visiting their website. We consider it an honor to walk alongside HADI in their mission to invest in people worldwide.

IMAG History and Science Center: Sparking Discovery

- **3,400+ New Website Visitors Monthly**
- **9% Average Monthly Click Through Rate**
- **40,000 Average Monthly Impressions**

The IMAG History and Science Center offers fun and enriching experiences for all ages, offering over 60 hands-on exhibits showcasing the wonders of science and history. From 3D movies about the animals of the Ice Age, to virtual reality trips back in time, to a 3,200+ gallon aquarium, IMAG sparks imagination and a passion for science and history in young visitors.

IMAG & Nonprofit Megaphone became partners in 2019. At that time, NPM helped to get the word out for their birthday parties and museum memberships. Hundreds of new people learning about what the IMAG has to offer led to more tickets being purchased, more events being booked, and more young people exposed to the magic of scientific and historical inquiry.

IMAG has continued to thrive during the Covid-19 era with the help of Google Ads to promote their IMAG@HOME online educational programming, instruction, and entertainment. Throughout 2020 and 2021, they continued to see over 3,400 new visitors to their website with an average click-through-rate of over 9%. We are so excited to come alongside IMAG and partner with them to promote their exciting history and science programs for all ages.

ENVIRONMENTAL NONPROFIT CASE STUDIES

Earthwatch Institute: Engaging the Science of Sustainability

- **6,300+ New People Engaging with Earthwatch's Website per Month**
- **8.30% Click Through Rate on Ads**
- **28 Expedition Signups, Each Driving $1.5-3.5k Revenue**

The Earthwatch Institute (earthwatch.org) is an international organization that brings people together with leading scientists to provide hands-on environmental research and education. Instead of simply reading academic articles, Earthwatch gives individuals the opportunity to participate in sustainability field research themselves, allowing them to see the impact of their efforts firsthand.

This brilliant model is executed in part through Earthwatch's "Expeditions," which fuse adventure and scientific inquiry. Website visitors are invited to sign up for Expeditions ranging from studying "Birdsongs in the Olympic Peninsula" to "Reforestation in Brazil." Participants pay to take part in these excursions, which makes the program both environmentally sustainable and financially sustainable. Earthwatch partnered with Nonprofit Megaphone to use the Google Ad Grant to reach an increasingly global audience in support of its global mission.

> *"We wanted a partner that could take the reins and move the strategy forward and come to the table with some ideas on how to improve the overall strategy . . . NPM has been a true partner who makes recommendations that they think would improve our end goals. It feels like they're a part of the team."*
>
> — *Kyle Gaw, Digital Marketing Director*

The results so far have been exceptional. In addition to great awareness, the Google Ad Grant ads are directly leading to Excursion bookings. With each booking representing $1.5k to $3.5k in revenue for Earthwatch, the financial ROI has been exceptional. But over the long term, the environmental ROI these programs help generate will be even greater.

Solar Sister: Investing in women. Powering the future.

- **1,766 Average Monthly Clicks**
- **3,000% Percentage Increase in Traffic**
- **7.74% Click Through Rate on Ads**

Solar Sister envisions a brighter world powered by women entrepreneurs, and they drive impact by investing in women-owned clean energy businesses in off-grid communities. In sub-Saharan Africa, where more than 600 million people have no access to electricity and over 700 million must rely on harmful fuels, Solar Sister believes women are a key part of the solution to the clean energy challenge.

Solar Sister empowers African women with economic opportunity, providing essential services and training that enable women entrepreneurs to build sustainable businesses.

THE NPM DIFFERENCE

Before coming to Nonprofit Megaphone, Solar Sister was struggling to generate new website traffic with only 43 monthly clicks to their site. They were unable to take advantage of the Google Ad Grant due to the complexities and time constraints of Google Ad management.

Since the start of working with NPM in September of 2020, they have seen a dramatic increase in traffic to their website. Within four months, the clicks to their site had gone up to 1,790.

Solar Sister shared,

"Since working with Nonprofit Megaphone, we have seen a huge increase in monthly clicks. Our average has increased by more than 3000%, and we have gotten as many as 2,322 clicks in one month. Many more new visitors are coming to our site. I was impressed to learn that 75% of the Ads that NPM posted are at the top of the Google search results in the first two or three slots.

We've been impressed by the attentive service and willingness to provide information that helps us understand. This is one thing that made Nonprofit Megaphone stand out from others."

SOLAR SISTER'S IMPACT

To date, over 7,000 Solar Sister Entrepreneurs have reached more than three million people with clean energy access. Products sold by Solar Sister Entrepreneurs have eliminated over 946,763 metric tonnes of CO_2 emissions. The training that Solar Sister provides gives women concrete tools to build their businesses and strategize.

The Google Ad Grant continues to bring increased awareness to their programs, and we are honored to partner with amazing organizations like Solar Sister. They remain dedicated to making an incredible difference for families in African communities while empowering women to light the way.

Textile Exchange: Creating Material Change

- **9,600+ New Website Visitors Monthly**
- **9.89% Click Through Rate on Ads**
- **80,000 Average Monthly Impressions**

Textile Exchange is a global non-profit that is making a difference in the world through its mission to minimize the harmful impact of the global textile industry and maximize its positive effects. They work tirelessly to fulfill this mission and now have staff and ambassadors in 11 countries and more than 25 countries represented as members.

In keeping with their mission, Textile Exchange provides a wealth of information – helping companies take advantage of numerous opportunities, alerting them to adjusting requirements in textile sustainability, and helping the industry to create real and lasting change. Partnering with Nonprofit Megaphone and taking advantage of the Google Ad Grant, Textile Exchange made huge strides in the amount of traffic that visited their website, adding an additional 9,600 people each month using the Grant.

Each of these new people then have the opportunity to learn more and engage with Textile Exchange in a wide variety of ways. Plus, this added exposure is a further incentive for the organization's corporate partners to continue using organic and environmentally conscious materials. The people have spoken, and they are about their fabrics!

American Orchid Society: Education. Conservation. Research.

- **$20,000+ Revenue Generated from Grant Ads**
- **150% Return on Investment**
- **2 Million Impressions across Google & Microsoft**

A Global Champion For Orchidaceae.

For over 100 years, the American Orchid Society has provided the most comprehensive information about orchid culture on the planet and continues to be a leading supporter of orchid research and conservation worldwide. The AOS envisions a world where orchids are protected, cultivated, and enjoyed. From the award-winning Orchids magazine to free educational webinars, the AOS is the ideal resource for orchid growers everywhere.

THE NPM DIFFERENCE

As an abundant source of information, the American Orchid Society needed a way to disseminate its resources to the right people. Seeking to expand its reach and visibility, the AOS team knew that the Google Ad Grant was the perfect tool to help accomplish this goal. Knowing that it would take the help of experts to properly manage the Google Ad Grant, The American Orchid Society partnered with Nonprofit Megaphone.

From the beginning of our partnership, the AOS has received thousands of monthly website visitors from Google Grant Ads. After seeing the success from the Google Ad Grant, the AOS decided to expand its reach even further by adding the Microsoft Ads for Social Impact Ad Grant to its management services. Thanks to the Microsoft Grant's inclusion of display ads, in only 6 months, their Microsoft ads generated 1 million impressions!

Between the 2 grants, the American Orchid Society's ads have been seen by over 2 million people! This success has inspired the AOS to invest in refreshing their website and content as a way to enhance their success even further. AOS knows that strong content is key to making the most of both sponsored and organic website traffic.

When asked about their partnership with NPM, Membership & Marketing Committee Chair William Bodei had this to say:

"The American Orchid Society wholeheartedly endorses NPM as a great partner. The investment pays for itself, and the analytics NPM provides has helped us improve our content and reach a much larger audience than ever before."

NPM is thrilled to help the American Orchid Society grow its reach through our continued partnership. It is an honor to partner with nonprofit organizations to amplify their voices.

HEALTH NONPROFIT CASE STUDIES

Nurse Practitioner Associates for Continuing Education: Keeping Care Cutting Edge

- **3,500+ New People Engaging with NPACE's Website per Month**
- **7.71% Click Through Rate on Ads**
- **30+ People Taking Action to Learn More About CE**

The Nurse Practitioner Associates for Continuing Education (NPACE) provides continuing education for nurse practitioners and other advanced practice clinicians all over the country. Their services include high quality, evidence-based educational programs that are accredited by the American Nurses Credentialing Center's Commission on Accreditation.

NPACE hosts conferences and online workshops throughout the year, providing specialized content and expert faculty. These conferences not only encourage growth in higher-level thinking and quality care for patients, but also provide networking opportunities for hundreds of primary care providers and nurse practitioners.

Since partnering with Nonprofit Megaphone for Google Ad Grant management the number of conversions NPACE is seeing has skyrocketed. Over one third of visitors from ads take action to learn more about registering for one or more continuing education offerings, and their click-through rate is steadily staying around 7.71%.

Hillcrest Hope: Changing Lives One Family at a Time

The Challenge

Though the team at Hillcrest Hope already had the Google Ad Grant, they were experiencing difficulty with effectively managing existing ad groups and campaigns according to best practice standards. They were also struggling to utilize data and reporting in guiding their overall marketing efforts.

The Outcome

By gaining an understanding of the overall mission and goals of Hillcrest Hope, NPM continues to help them further achieve their mission by promoting their services to a much larger audience.

- **1,100+ New People Engaging with the Website Monthly**
- **9.26% Click Through Rate on Ads**
- **12,500+ Average Monthly Impressions**

Hillcrest Hope offers a variety of services to struggling families in the Kansas City communities. They have provided the opportunity of housing and stability to many individuals and families for over four decades. Their three programs include Hope Essentials, two Clay County housing sites with the capacity to serve 21 families at one time; Hope Opportunities, an incentive-based support program for graduates; and Hope Solutions, an eviction prevention program.

In addition to their programs, the Hillcrest Hope Thrift Store is an integral part of their mission. All proceeds from the Thrift Store support their programs, and donations to the store directly help the families in need during their stay at Hillcrest Hope as well as upon graduation when they are seeking their own housing. NPM has seen tremendous success in promoting the thrift store through Google Ads, bringing greater awareness to the programs at Hillcrest Hope.

> *"NPM has given the attention to become so familiar with what we do and their work accurately reflects Hillcrest. They give us insight into how our ads are performing and share opportunities to communicate things in a different way or push things through social media."*
>
> — Rachel Hollinberger, Program and Marketing Director

Nonprofit Megaphone is thrilled to build strategic Google Ad campaigns with Hillcrest Hope to help make these services known to the local community. The creative keywords and original ad groups designed by the expert grant managers at Nonprofit Megaphone have driven more than 1,162 new visitors on a monthly basis, maintaining a click-through-rate of 9.26%. NPM is excited to continue to work alongside Hillcrest Hope to provide these opportunities to families in need.

Spotting Cancer: Spotting Cancer Early Saves Lives

- **24,245 Clicks 3rd Quarter 2021**
- **7.62% Click Through Rate on Ads 3rd Quarter 2021**
- **322 Guides Downloaded 3rd Quarter 2021**

Spotting Cancer has one incredible objective – to save lives. They empower people every day by providing information and methods to monitor their bodies between checkups or screenings to help provide early detection of any cancer signs or symptoms.

Spotting Cancer's main focus is providing information to the public. Some of the information they provide includes learning how to obtain family cancer history to share with family members or healthcare professionals, discovering typical signs and symptoms associated with cancer, finding the proper screening and testing options for early cancer detection, and explaining the importance of having a medical team. Spotting Cancer is doing everything possible to get the word out about information that could be the difference between life and death.

With this incredible mission, Nonprofit Megaphone is thrilled to partner with Spotting Cancer to manage their Google Ads. In the 3rd Quarter of 2021, they had incredible results, with over 24,200 clicks and over 300 informational guides and charts downloaded from their website. This resulted in an average click-through-rate of 7.62%. NPM is excited to continue working alongside Spotting Cancer to help them reach their goals by managing their Google Ads.

Glaucoma Research Foundation: Fueling Research & Support

- **4,800+ New People Engaging with the Foundation's Website Monthly**
- **8.01% Click Through Rate on Ads**
- **60,500+ Average Monthly Impressions**

Glaucoma is a disease that damages the optic nerve and causes progressive blindness. The Glaucoma Research Foundation (glaucoma.org) was founded to improve the lives of people with glaucoma and fuel research to ultimately cure the disease. The Foundation provides educational resources for patients who may have been recently diagnosed, funds potentially ground-breaking research, and operates a 3-day conference called Glaucoma 360 that brings together the entire sector.

The Glaucoma Research Foundation partnered with Nonprofit Megaphone to utilize the Google Ad Grant to gain more exposure and engage with its audience on both the disease and the progress being made. Google Ads allow the Foundation to reach individuals where they are, as they use Google for information about the condition as well as treatment and cures.

Most encouraging are the people who arrive at glaucoma.org each month through ads and take a next step to get involved – downloading PDF resources, subscribing to email updates, and even donating. Nonprofit Megaphone is proud to partner with the Glaucoma Research Foundation to fight for a more hopeful future for all.

COPD Foundation: Supporting Community & Fighting for Cures

- **9,000+ New People Engaging with COPD Foundation Monthly**
- **300+ New People Using COPD's Risk Screener Monthly**
- **11.2% Conversion Rate from Ads**

The COPD Foundation supports individuals with Chronic Obstructive Pulmonary Disease (COPD), provides screening to detect undiagnosed cases, advocates for policy changes, and fuels research aimed at treatment and cures. The Foundation operates a unique online "COPD360social" community of over 35,000 members globally who have COPD.

The COPD Foundation had a variety of messages that, if heard more broadly, could potentially save lives. One of these initiatives was encouraging individuals to take the Foundation's free, five question screener to detect risk for COPD. By partnering with Nonprofit Megaphone and utilizing the Google Ad Grant, the COPD Foundation has been able to drive an additional 300+ screenings completed per month through ads alone. Google Ads also support the Foundation's efforts to reach out to individuals with COPD, prompting dozens to join the COPD360social online community. This is in addition to the thousands of people who are visiting the COPD Foundation's website each month through Google Ads and engaging with all of the various offerings and services that are provided.

It is a rare privilege to run ad campaigns that may in some way save or enhance lives. All of us at Nonprofit Megaphone are thrilled to partner with the COPD Foundation on this critical work.

HUMAN & CIVIL RIGHTS NONPROFIT CASE STUDIES

YWCA Metropolitan Chicago: Eliminating Racism and Empowering Women

- **1,716 Clicks**
- **16,442 Impressions**
- **10.44% Click Through Rate on Ads**

YWCA Metropolitan Chicago is committed to eliminating racism, empowering women, and promoting peace, justice, freedom, and dignity for all. As a leading affiliate among a national network of more than 200 YWCAs, YWCA Metropolitan Chicago impacts tens of thousands of women and families annually through comprehensive human services provided across the region.

YWCA Metropolitan Chicago is a leading provider in the areas of sexual violence support services, early childhood services, Youth STEAM education, and economic empowerment services. Additionally, through the Until Justice Just Is initiative, they offer resources and specific action steps to advance racial justice.

Nonprofit Megaphone is thrilled to work with YWCA Metropolitan Chicago to promote their services, events, and workshops with the Google Ad Grant. Their account grows by leaps and bounds each month due to their great content and our expert grant management. Last month alone, their ads received more than 1,700 clicks with a CTR of 10.44%. We love seeing results like these and are thankful for the role we play in helping them advance their mission and make a positive impact.

YWCA USA: Eliminating Racism, Empowering Women

- **32,000+ Avg. Monthly Ad Impressions**
- **40 Avg. Monthly Donations Generated from Ads**
- **8.46% Click Through Rate**

YWCA USA is on a mission to eliminate racism, empower women, stand up for social justice, help families, and strengthen communities. We are one of the oldest and largest women's organizations in the nation, serving over 2 million women, girls, and their families.

YWCA has been at the forefront of the most pressing social movements for more than 160 years — from voting rights to civil rights, from affordable housing to pay equity, from violence prevention to health care reform. Today, we combine programming and advocacy in order to generate institutional change in three key areas: racial justice and civil rights, empowerment and economic advancement of women and girls, and health and safety of women and girls.

YWCA USA leverages Nonprofit Megaphone and the Google Ad Grant to reach its national audience to promote brand awareness and advocate for racial justice and empowerment for women. Current ad campaigns touch on topics such as ending racial profiling and the criminalization of people of color, as well as supporting girls of color who are trauma survivors.

Global Exchange: Building People-to-People Ties

- **5,000+ New People Engaging with the Website Monthly**
- **8.37% Click Through Rate on Ads**
- **60,000+ Monthly Impressions**

Global Exchange is an international human rights organization dedicated to promoting social, economic and environmental justice around the world. With such a timely mission, Global Exchange seeks to create change through education and their action resource center.

They also envision alternative economics that actively works to protect international human rights.

Founded over 30 years ago, they have seen many accomplishments, including helping to build the Fair Trade Movement, monitoring elections in Columbia, Mexico, and the U.S., and building the largest sustainability event (Green Festival) in the country. Within the last year, they launched a webcast series entitled Voices for Global Justice which brings together movement leaders, experts and organizers from around the world.

> *"The viewership of our webcast series highlighting human rights issues has increased a lot in part to Google Ads. It has been great seeing new names and faces tuning into our Voices for Global Justice webcasts."*
>
> — *Corina Nolet, Co-Executive Director*

It's been such a pleasure to partner with Global Exchange in their quest to promote social and economic justice around the world. During the last month, they had over 5,000 clicks from ads to their website and their ads were seen over 60,000 times. We are thrilled to be partnering with Global Exchange to share their story and build social justice around the world.

The Greenlining Institute: Removing Barriers to Opportunity

- **4,000+ Monthly New Visitors from Ads**
- **6.37% Click Through Rate on Ads**
- **125+ Reports Downloaded Monthly**

A champion for racial justice and equality, the Greenlining Institute is a policy, research, organizing, and leadership institute. Founded in

1993 and headquartered in California, the Institute brings together leaders from the community along with the public and private sector to affect change in policies and to open doors for opportunity.

Every program the Greenlining Institute takes on is fueled by a belief that the American Dream should be attainable for everyone. The Institute's Leadership Academy offers leaders of the future instruction and opportunities for success. Since 1996, the Academy has trained over 1,000 young leaders. Partnering with Nonprofit Megaphone to manage their Google Ad Grant is a key strategy to attract people to their website, increasing awareness for the Institute's programs and vision – "a nation where communities of color thrive and race is never a barrier to economic opportunity."

As a result of the partnership with Nonprofit Megaphone, The Greenlining Institute has welcomed over 4,000 new visitors to their website on a monthly basis.

HUMAN SERVICES NONPROFIT CASE STUDIES

Essential Partners: Build a Community Strengthened by Differences, Connected by Trust

- **2,300+ New Website Visitors Monthly**
- **7.55% Average Click Through Rate**
- **31,000 Impressions Monthly**

Essential Partners has spent more than 30 years equipping communities to live and work better together by building trust and understanding across differences. NPM began managing the Google Ad Grant for Essential Partners in August, 2017, and since that time, they have had over a million impressions and utilized more than $355,000 of the Google Ad Grant funds.

> *"NPM has been a great thought-partner as we redesigned and relaunched our website, helping restructure our campaigns to maximize our search traffic, addressing changes in Google search policies, and letting us track more goals. NPM has allowed Essential Partners to reach multitudes of people who would never have thought to look for us on their own."*
>
> — *Daniel Pritchard, Director of Strategic Communications*

NPM is encouraged to see the specific results of clients like Essential Partners. Their CTR, Spend, and Conversions metrics show that they're using the Google Ad Grant to reach out to key audience members. By engaging with these users, they grow their web presence and become available to the communities that need them!

Marine Raider Foundation: Helping Those Who Have Sacrificed the Most

- **800+ Clicks**
- **8.93% Click Through Rate on Ads**
- **10,700 Impressions**

Marine Raider Foundation provides support to active duty and medically retired United States Marine Forces Special Operations Command (MARSOC) Raiders and their families, as well as to the families of Raiders who have lost their lives in service to our nation. Seeking to help these families with assistance for needs that are unmet by the government, they work to help Raiders and their families make a full reintegration following wounds, injuries, and extended deployments.

The Marine Raider Foundation (MRF) utilizes four programs to help make their mission a reality. Through fundraisers and events offered throughout the year, they provide ongoing support to the MARSOC community with programs that include Raider Support, Family Resiliency, Tragedy Assistance & Survivor Support, and Raider Legacy & Preservation. Since May of 2012, the Marine Raider Foundation has provided over $4 million in support to MARSOC Marines, Sailors, and their families.

It's been exciting to work with Marine Raider Foundation in managing their Google Ads. They continue to keep a steady click-through-rate average of 9%, and 800+ new people are visiting their website each month.

> "The Foundation hosted a virtual challenge over the summer that ended up raising $112,000. We feel that the marketing provided in the ads created by Nonprofit Megaphone played a role in bringing the challenge to the attention of a wider audience, which in turn led to the success of the event."
>
> — Sarah Christian, Director of Operations

Partnering with Marine Raider Foundation has been a pleasure, but being witness to their dedication to the MARSOC community during the COVID crisis has been especially meaningful. Due to the pandemic, they worked tirelessly to transition to virtual events and fundraisers to ensure their community had the resources they needed when they needed them most. For us, it was an honor to work alongside them in helping them raise the necessary funds. We are thrilled to continue managing the Google Ad Grant for Marine Raider Foundation and look forward to the incredible results to come.

Goodwill of Central NC: Empowering Local Employment

- **500+ New People Engaging with the Website Monthly**
- **13.13% Click Through Rate on Ads**
- **13.07% Of Visitors from Ads Taking Action on the Website**

The Goodwill of Central North Carolina, also known as Triad Goodwill, is a leader in the nonprofit industry. Underlying everything they do is the mission to promote the value of work by providing career development services and work opportunities for people with employment needs. And they are knocking it out of the park!

In the year 2017-2018, they served over 13,500 people in surrounding counties and helped over 2,700 job seekers find employment. This thriving nonprofit provides these service opportunities by donating 85 cents for every dollar that is spent at its retail stores.

It's no wonder that when they partnered with Nonprofit Megaphone to manage their Google Ad Grant, they saw continued growth in the form of donations! In the first month alone, the donation pick-up requests increased so much that they suggested their ads for donations be reduced. In the words of the client, "It seems that your efforts to promote donation pickups have really worked!" With almost 500 new people engaging with their website each month, they have also seen a 13.07% conversion rate, allowing more people in the community to support the mission and vision of the Goodwill of Central North Carolina.

Kendal at Oberlin: Transforming the Experience of Aging

- **6,500+ Daily New Website Visitors**
- **7.73% Click Through Rate**
- **84,000+ Average Monthly Impressions**

Kendal at Oberlin is a community focused on healthy aging, serving residents who have come from across the country (36 states and Washington DC are represented). Founded in 1993, the facility has become a hub for recreation and fellowship, offering a fitness center open to the community, musical performances, and additional programs such as Kendal at Home and the Kendal Early Learning Program.

Searching for a retirement community for a loved one is typically a lengthy and wide-ranging process. With 40% of all residents coming from outside of OH, Kendal at Oberlin needed a way to reach a wider audience that might not be aware of their unique approach to aging and care.

Nonprofit Megaphone and the Google Ad Grant allow Kendal at Oberlin to appear in the most valuable marketing real estate in this search process: at the top of the results during Google searches. Prospective residents and families almost always conduct their searches online, and having the funds to invest in placing ads ensures Kendal at Oberlin can meet folks where they are, and encourage them to learn more.

In a unique partnership, Nonprofit Megaphone collaborated with Marketing Essentials, which provides content for the Kendal website for inbound marketing that is further amplified by the Google Ad Grant spend. This collaboration allows Kendal at Oberlin to receive even more benefit from the Ad Grant program.

Penn-Mar Human Services: Transforming Life Into Living

- **200+ Conversions**
- **5.87% Click-Through Rate on Ads**
- **1,700+ New Website Visitors Monthly**

As Gregory Miller, President & CEO of Penn-Mar Human Services puts it, "A life of purpose and meaning is our goal for individuals with intellectual disabilities." Penn-Mar serves over 400 adults with intellectual disabilities through a wide variety of programs. From employment support to educational opportunities, community based programs to residential and respite opportunities, Penn-Mar holistically addresses the needs of the individual and community.

> *"We have been very pleased with the results of our collaboration with Nonprofit Megaphone. In the brief amount of time we have worked with the team, we have already seen a substantial increase in website visitors and have learned so much from their expertise. We value their insights, creativity, and their commitment to the success of Penn-Mar Human Services."*
>
> *— Matthew Muench Penn-Mar Human Services*

FAITH & RELIGION NONPROFIT CASE STUDIES

Book of Mormon Central: Making the Book of Mormon Accessible

- **5,200+ New People Engaging with the Website Monthly**
- **11.48% Click Through Rate on Ads**
- **45,000+ Average Monthly Impressions**

Book of Mormon Central (BMC) exists every day to make the Book of Mormon accessible, comprehensible, and defensible to the entire world. Their incredible team of experts works together to share the wonder of the Book of Mormon with the world.

As an independent organization operating with the Book of Mormon Archaeological Forum, BMC's mission statement is to increase understanding and faithful engagement with the Book of Mormon. There are a variety of ways they do this, and two of their most effective are ScripturePlus and KnoWhys. ScripturePlus is a fully-interactive scripture study app designed to encourage learners to engage in the Word of God more fully. KnowWhys are concise, media-enriched articles that explain difficult topics, interesting insights, and more in the Book of Mormon.

> *"Since partnering with NPM, user engagements are up 70% and donations are up 55%. NPM has helped us publicize a weekly YouTube show that is now attracting 100k views. About a year ago, we launched a new website and let it grow organically. Since NPM began driving traffic to it a couple months ago, pageviews are up 75%."*
>
> — *Kirk Magleby, Executive Director, Book of Mormon Central*

NPM is so excited to see tangible results as we work with our clients! Book of Mormon Central is now receiving over 45,000 impressions monthly, and over 5,200 people are visiting their website! That is a fantastic use of the Google Ad Grant!

Paul Tripp Ministries: Connecting the Transforming Power of Jesus Christ to Everyday Life

- **15,900+ Clicks**
- **6.71% Click Through Rate on Ads**
- **237,150+ Impressions**

Paul Tripp Ministries is an international organization focused on connecting the transforming power of Jesus Christ to everyday life by posting online content, writing books, producing teaching series, and speaking at events around the world. Dr. Paul David Tripp, founder, has planted a church, founded a Christian school, written worship songs, and toured with a Christian band. He was a faculty member at the Christian Counseling and Educational Foundation (CCEF) for many years, a lecturer in Biblical Counseling at Westminster Theological Seminary, a Visiting Professor at Southern Baptist Theological Seminary, and a pastor at Tenth Presbyterian Church.

Paul Tripp Ministries offers a variety of free services to share the Word of God. Bible studies, sermons, articles, podcasts, videos, and a mobile app share resources on topics including marriage, parenting, evangelism, suffering, doctrine, and more. Additionally, the ministry has an e-commerce store where books, e-books, audiobooks, group study resources, video lessons, and conference videos can be purchased.

Nonprofit Megaphone is proud to work with Paul Tripp Ministries to help them spread the Word by reaching a global audience through effective Google Ad Grant management.

> *"In just two years of working with NPM, they literally 10Xed our clicks and impressions from ads. We went from 1,500 clicks in October of 2018 to 15,000 clicks in October of 2020. Monthly impressions rose from 20,000 to 208,000. We're gaining new visitors, subscribers, app downloads, store customers, and even donors from around the world."*
>
> — Ben Fallon, Marketing & Communications

Last month alone, their ads received over 15,916 clicks with a CTR of 6.71%. Furthermore, 366 visitors who arrived on the website after clicking on an ad completed a meaningful conversion such as downloading a sermon, signing up for Wednesday's Devotional, or downloading their mobile app. It has been incredible watching their account grow over time and knowing that in doing so, people around the world are growing in their faith and finding comfort in the Word.

Hillel International: Enriching the Lives of Jewish Students

- **5,700+ New People Engaging with Hillel per Month**
- **7.5% Average Click Through Rate**
- **320+ Ecards Sent + New Email Subscribers per Month**

Hillel International serves hundreds of thousands of Jewish college students globally, providing impactful and distinctly Jewish experiences and opportunities. As a result, 94% of the students Hillel serves say that being Jewish will continue to be important to them after graduation.

Since Hillel's audience contains a large number of tech-savvy students, reaching them online is a critical component of Hillel's engagement strategy. Hillel partnered with Nonprofit Megaphone to utilize the Google Ad Grant to get in front of this audience in a cost-effective and scalable way. With campaigns supporting initiatives ranging from

Hillel's guide to colleges from a Jewish perspective to ads boosting awareness of Jewish holidays, Hillel shares it's content via the Google Ad Grant with thousands of visitors each month.

Even more powerfully, Hillel's highly optimized website and eCard program provide the organization an effective method of converting visitors into email list subscribers, which Hillel can then nurture into donors over the long term.

Forgotten Children Worldwide: Marketing to a National Audience

- **2,300+ Average New Monthly Website Visitors from the Google Grant**
- **6.23% Click-Through Rate on Ads**
- **150 Conversions**

Forgotten Children Worldwide has a clear mission: protecting the most vulnerable orphans and children from the evils of abandonment, poverty, and human trafficking. The organization is truly global in scope, working with partners on the ground in India, Kenya, Malawi, Nepal, Uganda and Zimbabwe. Children face a variety of issues, and Forgotten Children Worldwide has a comprehensive set of programs to provide truly holistic solutions, including:

- Child Sponsorship
- Clothing Distribution
- Construction Projects
- Water and Wellness
- Self-Sustainability Initiatives

Jeff Patterson, the Director of Development, came from a career in radio and knew the importance of reaching a broad audience. With Nonprofit Megaphone and the Google Ad Grant, he is able to promote sponsorship programs and other initiatives across the country, raising the profile of his organization and building brand awareness. With more than 2,000 new people learning about Forgotten Children's work through the Ad Grant each month, representing nearly over 67% of total website traffic, this is one of the most effective marketing channels for expanding the nonprofit's impact.

> *"Working with Nonprofit Megaphone has allowed us to expand our reach all over the U.S. They keep us up-to-date on grant requirements & are always willing to help us figure out ways to get more conversions. Their partnership is an ongoing part of our marketing strategy and their team is great to work with."*
>
> *— Jeff Patterson, Director of Development, Forgotten Children Worldwide*

SPORTS & ATHLETICS NONPROFIT CASE STUDIES

Chicago Area Runners Association: Helping Everyone "Go Run"!

- **5,800+ New People Engaging with the Website Monthly**
- **13.77% Click Through Rate on Ads**
- **25%+ Of All Website Traffic from the Google Grant**

The Chicago Area Runners Association (CARA) began in 1978 as a grassroots organization, and stays true to those roots. Today, CARA boasts over 10,000 members, who collectively volunteer over 42,000 hours each year to facilitate the organization's programs.

As the third largest community of local runners in the United States, CARA was looking for a way to engage new people in the organization's mission and get them involved in events, races, and training opportunities. Working with Nonprofit Megaphone, the Chicago Area Runners Association has gone from a standing start to spending over $8,000 of the Google Ad Grant each month and bringing nearly 5,500 new people to the website on a monthly basis.

This fantastic performance has built over time, showcasing the value of continuing to invest in building momentum with the Google Ad Grant. All of us at Nonprofit Megaphone are thrilled to be partnering with CARA and look forward to breaking new "personal records" together.

U.S. Masters Swimming: Driving Adult Fitness

- **5,800+ New People Engaging with the Website Monthly**
- **10.51% Click Through Rate on Ads**
- **380+ Monthly Conversions**

U.S. Masters Swimming officially began May 2, 1970, after Captain Ransom J. Arthur, M.D., a Navy doctor in San Diego, convinced John Spannuth, then president of the Coaches Association, to hold the first National Masters Swimming Championships in the Amarillo Aquatic Club pool. Arthur felt that if the incentive was appealing, it would give older swimmers (ex-competitors and beginners alike) a goal for keeping physically fit. Dr. Arthur's vision of adults improving their fitness through swimming has grown over the years into a nationwide organization of nearly 60,000 adult swimmers.

U.S. Masters Swimming encourages adults to enjoy the health, fitness, and social benefits of swimming by providing more than 2,000 adult swimming programs and events across the country, including open water and pool competitions. USMS's nearly 70,000 members range from age 18 to 99 and include swimmers of all ability levels. During the midst of the COVID-19 pandemic, it was certainly much harder for adults to participate in and take advantage of all that USMS had to offer. USMS wanted to make sure their members were still feeling connected and had access to information to help get them through that tough time. They did this by providing more than 40 articles on drylands training, mental health, open water swimming, coronavirus and swimming, and many more. One of their articles had over 700,000 views! They also created the first-ever virtual swim meet!

NPM is proud to to manage the Google Ads for USMS and has partnered with them for over four years. They continue to maintain an average click-through-rate of 10%, which is far above Google's required 5%. They also average over 5,800 new visitors to their website monthly. We are excited to see how expert management of their Google Ads continue to bring new visitors to their website and new members to their organization. And we love that the feeling is mutual. When asked what their experience has been working with NPM,

> *"It's like letting a dog-lover watch your dog while you are away and can't take proper care of it."*
>
> — Kyle Deery, Senior Director, Marketing and Communications

National Sports Center: Beyond the Bench!

- **3,500+ New People Engaging with the Website Monthly**
- **13.07% Click Through Rate on Ads**
- **200+ Conversions from Ads**

National Sports Center The National Sports Center, also known as the world's largest amateur sports facility, operates over 100 unique programs and events in a variety of sports. They also host many national and international competitions, drawing over 4 million visitors each year.

The NSC has two missions. The first is to provide amateur sports opportunities to Minnesota residents. On an average day, there are 12 different programs and events taking place at the NSC and most are serving the local community. The second is to generate out-of-state economic impact through amateur sports events and programs. These special events generate over $83 million in annual visitor economic impact.

Nonprofit Megaphone is excited to partner with the NSC. The NSC is in its third year with NPM, taking advantage of their grant management expertise. Since joining with NPM, the NSC has had over 140,000 new visitors to their website and maintained a click-through-rate of

13.07%. NPM is proud to come alongside sports organizations such as the National Sports Center to advance their great mission!

SIAC: Doing it Big!

- **4,700+ New People Engaging with the Website Monthly**
- **7.69% Click Through Rate on Ads**
- **62,000+ Impressions from Ads**

SIAC The Southern Intercollegiate Athletic Conference (SIAC) is a NCAA athletic conference consisting primarily of historically black colleges and universities. Headquartered in downtown Atlanta, Georgia, this conference began in December 1913 and is now in its 106th year, supporting 14 institutions across a contiguous six-state footprint.

Empowering students, schools, and communities, the SIAC sponsors seven men's championships (baseball, basketball, cross country, football, golf, outdoor track & field, and tennis) and six women's championships (basketball, cross country, outdoor track & field, softball, tennis, and volleyball).

The SIAC is coming up on a year of partnering with NPM to manage their Google Grant, with some exciting results! Over the last month, they have had over 4,700 first-time visitors to their website while enjoying a click-through-rate of 7.69%. With top-notch grant managers keeping their keywords relevant and up-to-date, they had over 62,000 impressions in that same month. NPM enjoys working with nonprofits like the SIAC, helping them to allow student athletes competitive intercollegiate opportunities.

YOUTH NONPROFIT CASE STUDIES

The Boy Scouts of America: Prepared. For Life.

- **500 Estimated New Members Annually**
- **19,605 Average Monthly Clicks**
- **25.16% Average Click-Through-Rate on Ads**

The mission of the Boy Scouts of America (BSA) is to prepare young people to make ethical and moral choices throughout their lives by instilling in them the values of the Scout Oath and Law. Scouting encourages youth to strive to do their best for their God and country, to help others, and emphasizes the importance of maintaining good physical, moral, and mental conditions. Discovery is at the heart of all Scouting programs. Scouting equips youth of all ages from diverse backgrounds to explore a variety of topics and ideas, in addition to preparing them for a lifetime of service and leadership. From Cub Scouts, to Boy Scouts, Venturers, Sea Scouts, and Explorers, there are Scouting programs for all ages, backgrounds, and interests.

THE NPM DIFFERENCE

Scouting teaches youth to face any challenge in life. After all, the Scout Motto is "Be Prepared." In 2020, the national BSA was being challenged by a decline in membership enrollment, and budget constraints presented an additional difficulty. They partnered with Nonprofit Megaphone in order to build awareness of their programs and to leverage the search features of Google through the Google Ad Grant.

Through NPM-managed Google ads, BSA has generated renewed interest in their programs receiving an average of nearly 20,000 clicks per month and a yearly average of 1,500 new membership leads. They estimate 30% of those actually join, leading to 500 new memberships each year! They come close to spending the full $10,000 grant each month, with an average monthly Click-Through-Rate of 25.16%, and increased awareness of niche events like Jamboree and High Adventure Bases.

When asked about his experiences with NPM and the Google Ad Grant, Thomas Rugh, Team Lead for National Marketing stated:

"I would encourage any non profit to work with NPM. In my 12 years at BSA this is the best ROI (Return On Investment) program that we have."

NPM is honored to help BSA overcome their challenges and looks forward to continuing to be a part of their growth and success. It is a joy to be able to help our clients spread awareness of their programs and foster new growth.

Glossary of Key Terms

When working with Google Ads and the Google Ad Grant, it's essential to familiarize yourself with the key terminology used in the platform. Understanding these terms will help you navigate the interface, set up campaigns effectively, and communicate with others in the field. Let's dive into the most important terms you should know:

A/B Testing: The practice of comparing two or more variations of an ad, landing page, or other element to determine which version performs better based on metrics like click-through rate or conversion rate.

Account Structure: The way you organize your campaigns, ad groups, and keywords within your Google Ads account to ensure relevance, efficiency, and ease of management.

Ad Approval Process: The review process Google undertakes to ensure that all ads meet their advertising policies before being displayed to users.

Ad Auction: The process Google uses to determine which ads to show for a particular search query. Factors include the advertiser's bid, the quality and relevance of the ad, and the expected impact of the ad.

Ad Delivery Method: The way Google Ads distributes your budget throughout the day. Options include standard delivery (evenly over time) and accelerated delivery (as quickly as possible).

Ad Extension: Additional pieces of information that can be added to your ads to provide more context and improve visibility, such as sitelinks, callouts, or phone numbers.

Ad Group: A collection of ads and keywords within a campaign that share similar themes or targets.

Ad Position: The order in which your ad appears on the search results page relative to other ads. Ad position is determined by your Ad Rank.

Ad Rank Threshold: The minimum Ad Rank required for your ad to be displayed in a particular position on the search results page. Ad Rank thresholds are based on factors like the quality and relevance of the ads competing for the same position.

Ad Rank: The position of your ad on the search results page, determined by your bid and Quality Score. Higher Ad Ranks lead to better visibility and more clicks.

Ad Rotation: The way Google Ads alternates between displaying different ads within an ad group. Options include optimizing for clicks, optimizing for conversions, or rotating evenly.

Ad Schedule: The days and times when your ads are set to appear. Ad scheduling allows you to control when your ads are shown based on your target audience's behavior and your organization's goals.

Ad Strength: An indicator that provides feedback on the quality and effectiveness of your responsive search ads, helping you optimize your ad content for better performance.

Attribution: The process of determining which ads, keywords, or campaigns are responsible for driving conversions or other desired actions on your website.

Audience Targeting: The practice of showing your ads to specific groups of people based on factors like their interests, demographics, or past interactions with your website.

Bid Adjustment: A percentage change applied to your bids for specific targeting criteria, such as device type, location, or ad schedule, allowing you to fine-tune your bids based on performance.

Bidding Strategy: The method used to determine how much you'll pay for each click on your ad. Common bidding strategies include maximizing clicks, targeting a specific cost-per-acquisition (CPA), or focusing on ad visibility.

Call Extensions: An ad extension that allows you to display a clickable phone number with your ads, encouraging users to call your organization directly.

Callout Extensions: An ad extension that allows you to highlight unique selling points, features, or benefits of your nonprofit organization in short, bullet-point phrases below your ad text. Callout extensions can help improve ad visibility and provide additional information to users without requiring them to click through to your website.

Campaign: The highest level of organization in Google Ads, typically used to group ad groups and keywords related to a common theme, product, or goal.

Click Share: The percentage of total possible clicks that your ads receive for a given keyword or set of keywords.

Click-Through Rate (CTR): The percentage of people who click on your ad after seeing it. A higher CTR generally indicates that your ad is relevant and compelling to users.

Conversion Rate: The percentage of users who complete a desired action (conversion) after clicking on your ad.

Conversion Window: The period after an ad click during which a conversion can be attributed to that click. Default conversion windows are typically 30 days for most conversion types.

Conversion: A desired action that a user takes on your website after clicking on your ad, such as making a donation, signing up for a newsletter, or completing a form.

Copywriting: The process of writing persuasive and compelling ad text that encourages users to click on your ad and take action on your website.

Cost-Per-Acquisition (CPA): The average amount you pay for each conversion generated by your ads.

Cost-Per-Click (CPC): The amount you pay each time someone clicks on your ad. In the Google Ad Grant program, the maximum CPC is $2.00 USD.

First-Page Bid Estimate: The approximate CPC bid needed for your ad to appear on the first page of Google search results for a particular keyword.

Frequency Capping: A setting that limits the number of times your ads are shown to the same user within a specified time period to avoid overexposure and ad fatigue.

Geographic Targeting: The practice of showing your ads to users in specific locations, such as countries, regions, cities, or even postal codes.

Google Ad Grant: A program that provides eligible nonprofit organizations with $10,000 USD per month in in-kind Google Ads advertising.

Google Ads Editor: A free, downloadable application that enables you to manage your Google Ads campaigns offline and make bulk changes to your accounts.

Google Ads: Google's online advertising platform that allows businesses and organizations to create and display ads on Google's search results pages and across its network of partner websites.

Google Analytics: A free web analytics tool that helps you track and analyze user behavior on your website, including traffic sources, page views, and conversions.

Google Tag Manager: A tag management system that allows you to easily add and update tracking codes (tags) on your website without modifying the code directly.

Image Extensions: An ad extension that allows you to display relevant images alongside your search ads, helping your ad stand out on the search results page and providing visual context for your message. Image extensions can be particularly effective for nonprofits, as they can showcase powerful visuals related to your cause or the impact of your work.

Impression Share: The percentage of impressions your ads receive compared to the total number of impressions they could potentially receive based on your targeting settings and budget.

Impressions: The number of times your ad is displayed, regardless of whether it is clicked on or not.

Keyword Match Types: The different ways you can specify how closely a user's search query must match your keyword for your ad to appear. Match types include broad match, phrase match, exact match, and negative match.

Keyword Planner: A tool within Google Ads that helps you research and discover new keywords, get bid estimates, and forecast campaign performance.

Keywords: Words or phrases that users enter into Google's search engine when looking for information, products, or services. Advertisers bid on keywords to trigger their ads to appear in search results.

Landing Page: The webpage where users are directed after clicking on your ad. Effective landing pages are relevant to the ad, load quickly, and provide a clear call-to-action (CTA).

Lost Impression Share: The percentage of potential impressions your ads missed out on due to factors like low Ad Rank, budget limitations, or targeting restrictions.

Monthly Budget: The amount of money you allocate to your Google Ads campaigns each month. For Google Ad Grant recipients, this is typically the $10,000 USD grant amount.

Negative Keywords: Words or phrases that you exclude from your campaigns to prevent your ads from showing for irrelevant or unwanted search queries.

Performance Metrics: The various data points used to measure the success and effectiveness of your Google Ads campaigns, such as clicks, impressions, CTR, CPC, and conversion rate.

Quality Score: A rating from 1-10 that Google assigns to each keyword in your ad campaigns, based on factors such as the relevance of your ad to the keyword, the expected click-through rate (CTR), and the quality of your landing page.

Remarketing: A strategy that allows you to show ads to people who have previously interacted with your website, helping you reconnect with interested audiences and encourage them to take action.

Responsive Search Ads: A type of search ad that automatically adapts its content to better match potential search queries, allowing you to create multiple headlines and descriptions that Google Ads will mix and match. These are now required by Google for all new search ad campaigns.

Return on Ad Spend (ROAS): A metric that measures the revenue generated for each dollar spent on advertising.

Sitelink Extensions: An ad extension that allows you to display additional links to specific pages on your website beneath your ad, providing users with more options and information.

Structured Snippet Extensions: An ad extension that allows you to highlight specific aspects of your nonprofit's services, programs, or offerings in a formatted list below your ad.

View-Through Conversion: A conversion that occurs when a user sees your ad (impression) but doesn't click on it, then later completes a desired action on your website.

Conclusion

If you've made it this far, thank you so much for investing your valuable time in learning about ways the Google Grant could help your nonprofit organization. I am so inspired by people like you who have an incredibly deep dedication to the cause they support and the communities they serve.

If we can ever be helpful for you at Nonprofit Megaphone in helping you maximize the impact of the Google Grant, it would be our honor. You can reach us at nonprofitmegaphone.com, and if you do reach out, let us know that you read this book and made it all the way to the end! That will absolutely make our day.

Whether you are a staff member, board member or volunteer, people like you make the world go round, often in unseen and insufficiently appreciated ways. It is our deep privilege to help people like you and organizations like yours in any way we can.

Made in the USA
Columbia, SC
24 June 2025